# Same-Sex Marriage

# Same-Sex Marriage

*Exploring the Issues*

Scott A. Merriman

*Religion in Politics and Society Today*

**ABC-CLIO®**

An Imprint of ABC-CLIO, LLC
Santa Barbara, California • Denver, Colorado

**Library of Congress Cataloging-in-Publication Data**

Names: Merriman, Scott A., 1968- author.
Title: Same-sex marriage : exploring the issues / Scott A. Merriman.
Description: Santa Barbara, California : ABC-CLIO, 2022. | Series: Religion in politics and society today | Includes bibliographical references and index.
Identifiers: LCCN 2021018941 (print) | LCCN 2021018942 (ebook) | ISBN 9781440875236 (hardcover; alk. paper) | ISBN 9781440875243 (ebook)
Subjects: LCSH: Same-sex marriage—United States—History.
Classification: LCC HQ1034.U5 M47 2022 (print) | LCC HQ1034.U5 (ebook) | DDC 306.84/80973—dc23
LC record available at https://lccn.loc.gov/2021018941
LC ebook record available at https://lccn.loc.gov/2021018942

ISBN: 978-1-4408-7523-6 (print)
      978-1-4408-7524-3 (ebook)

26   25   24   23   22      1   2   3   4   5

This book is also available as an eBook.

ABC-CLIO
An Imprint of ABC-CLIO, LLC

ABC-CLIO, LLC
147 Castilian Drive
Santa Barbara, California 93117
www.abc-clio.com

This book is printed on acid-free paper ∞

Manufactured in the United States of America

# Contents

# Alphabetical List of Entries

# Topical List of Entries

# Series Foreword

Religion is a pervasive and powerful force in modern society, and its influence on political structures and social institutions is inescapable, whether in the United States or around the world. Wars have been fought in the name of faith; national boundaries have been shaped as a result; and social policies, legislation, and daily life have all been shaped by religious beliefs. Written with the reference needs of high school students and undergraduates in mind, the books in this series examine the role of religion in contemporary politics and society. While the focus of the series is on the United States, it also explores social and political issues of global significance.

Each book in the series is devoted to a particular issue, such as anti-semitism, atheism and agnosticism, and women in Islam. An overview essay surveys the development of the religious dimensions of the subject and discusses how religion informs contemporary discourse related to that issue. A chronology then highlights the chief events related to the topic. This is followed by a section of alphabetically arranged reference entries providing objective information about people, legislation, ideas, movements, events, places, and other specific subjects. Each entry cites works for further reading and in many cases provides cross-references. At the end of each volume is an annotated bibliography of the most important print and electronic resources suitable for student research.

Authoritative and objective, the books in this series give readers a concise introduction to the dynamic interplay of religion and politics in modern society and provide a starting point for further research on social issues.

# Preface

The subject of same-sex marriage, including its intersection with the sub-ject of religion, has exploded onto the cultural and political scene in the last 50 years. Before 1970, no state acted to ban same-sex marriage. In fact, it was not until 1970 that a same-sex couple applied for (and was denied) a marriage license in the United States. Thus, nearly 200 years after our country was founded, the subject was not even on most people's radars. Now, just about 50 years later, same-sex marriage is legal across the United States.

Two things need to be considered here: first, the LGBTQ rights move-ment in general and how it led to a push for marriage equality, and second, the effect of religion in all of this. Before the late 1960s, there really was no public gay or lesbian rights movement in the United States. There were quiet efforts to educate the public and muted protests (in the early 1960s) against antigay actions, but nothing public. In 1969, the Stonewall riots marked the start of the modern movement. A police raid led to wide-scale protests, and the public took notice. In time, this led to more public notice of the gay and lesbian subculture in some cities and to the formation of a variety of gay liberation groups who aimed to publicly confront the repres-sion. The year 1970 saw the first Gay Pride Marches, and there was a sense that the situation was not going to be the same. During the 1970s, change occurred slowly, and there were many different firsts, such as the first Gay Pride March and the first gay pride group in a state or city, among others. Official treatment also started to change. In the 1970s, "homosexuality" was removed as a disease from the *Diagnostic and Statistical Manual of Mental Disorders* (DSM) used by professional psychologists.

Also, and very importantly, gay and lesbian men and women rejected the fear that they had been living with in the 1950s and 1960s. Gay and lesbian people in the 1950s and 1960s often wanted to be left alone to live quietly and to have their sexuality left alone; some later admitted to feeling guilty for being gay. By the 1970s, this attitude was largely rejected. Whether or not one wanted to be public about their sexuality varied, but the whole issue of shame was lessened, at least on behalf of many gay and lesbian men and women in the more metropolitan areas. This would be very important to the marriage equality movement, as pushing for marriage equality was very public.

The 1970s ended with a few pitched battles over LGBTQ rights. Harvey Milk was elected as the first openly gay city supervisor in San Francisco, and in Miami, there was a battle over an ordinance banning discrimination against gay people. Anita Bryant, a well-known singer, claimed the law threatened children. A pitched battle ensued, further mobilizing those in favor of LGBTQ rights. When Harvey Milk was killed and his killer received a light sentence, San Francisco erupted into riots—a public notice that the LGBTQ community was not going to accept homophobia anymore.

The 1980s saw the rise of AIDS in the United States, a disease that was discriminatorily linked with LGBTQ individuals. Many gay men realized that they had no rights in terms of their partners' wishes, and the religious right even claimed that AIDS was a plague sent by God as a punishment for a "sinful" lifestyle. All in all, many gay people felt forced to become active on the national scene. Before the 1980s, there were a few enclaves where gay men and women had some political power or were accepted, but they were generally nonexistent on the national scene. Gay and lesbian individuals (but mostly gay men, for a variety of reasons) had to organize and learn how to lobby in a crash course.

Gay men were more active in AIDS organizations because AIDS was more prevalent among gay men than lesbian women. Early AIDS organizations also replicated, unfortunately, the sexism in the larger society, with men being the leaders. In about seven years, national groups went from nearly nonexistent to persuading a large-scale research effort into finding a treatment for AIDS. This jolted many into political action, which continued into the next decade.

LGBTQ individuals faced another battle in the 1990s over gay and lesbians serving in the military. The old policy sought to force LGBTQ men and women out, but a variety of high-profile cases, such as those of Leonard Matlovich and Miriam Ben-Shalom, forced some of the military and the public to rethink this. On the other hand, conservatives were not yet willing to allow LGBTQ people to serve openly in the military. This led to the "Don't Ask, Don't Tell" policy, which allowed LGBTQ people to serve in the military but not openly. Neither side was happy with the compromise. By the 1990s, the LGBTQ community had grown increasingly vocal and politically active, and men and women were ready to start the battle over same-sex marriage.

Religion plays an important role in the same-sex marriage issue, and religion has been reenergized in the public sphere, or at least seems to have been reenergized. That is harder to determine. The United States believes itself to be a godly country, but few accurate surveys exist on religion. At the very least, many Americans believe themselves to be religious but are often somewhat quiet on religion. The debate over same-sex marriage, though, brought religion back to the fore. There were those who thought that religion would allow them to keep same-sex marriage banned, others who thought that religion should not be allowed to restrict their freedom, and still others who thought that the religion of those who wanted same-sex marriage banned was not their religion.

Religion has also played a role in marriage, but not as directly as most Americans think. While many Americans have been married in churches and other religious institutions throughout American history, marriage (and divorce) has always been a state institution in the United States, not a religious one. One could always get married at the courthouse, even if society may sometimes frown on it. Divorce was also an institution regulated by the state, not by the church. Unlike Henry VIII, no American had to get the permission of the pope to divorce, at least as far as the state was concerned. (One did have to get the church's permission for an annulment to marry again in the church.)

Religion was also seen as a bar to marriage. One was not supposed to marry outside of one's church. However, that was only, once again, in the eyes of the church, not the state. (Some public opinion also favored this, but it was generally not a legal issue.) Thus, while religious sentiment and public opinion played a part for many in the history of the United States, there were generally no legal bans on marriage due to religion.

However, the state, and religion somewhat, did play a role in one legal ban. Many states across the country had bans on marrying outside one's race. Some were bans on white people marrying Black people and vice versa, while others were bans on anyone nonwhite marrying a white person. These bans were often defended with religious reasons. Segregationists and those opposed to racial intermarriage argued that there was something in the Bible that defended segregation or that some sort of general separation of the races (perhaps in different countries) existed. Bans on interracial marriage existed until 1967 and the case of *Loving v. Virginia*, although some states kept the laws on the books or in their constitutions until the late 1990s and early 2000s. Religion also gave some people a bedrock against having to discuss the bans on interracial marriage. If religion banned something and religion was unchanging, the ban was unchanging as well. This would foreshadow an element in the battle over same-sex marriage.

Religion had also been a force in a previous battle over who could marry. For around 60 years in the 19th century, the Mormon religion had encouraged polygamy, particularly among its leaders. The Mormons were also largely in the Utah Territory. While it was under the federal government's authority, as a territory, the Mormons were largely able to rule their own area. However, when Utah wanted to become a state, the federal government moved to crack down on polygamy. As the bans were strengthened and cases prosecuted, it worked its way through the federal government until the U.S. Supreme Court heard the issue. In 1879, freedom of religion was held to not be a defense against polygamy. In the early 1890s, the Mormon Church changed its doctrine, holding polygamy now to be banned, and Utah was then admitted as a state in 1896. Some renegade offshoots of the Mormon Church still practice polygamy, but the main church opposes the practice.

Religion outside of the law has also played an important role in marriage. For years, many people would not marry those outside of their own religion. Others, while being *willing* to marry outside of their religion, *preferred* to marry inside it. Still a third group generally pushed outsider spouses to convert. All of this points to the strong role of religion in marriage, even while religion did not technically control the institution. This ties in with the topic of same-sex marriage, as religion played a large role in how a lot of people thought about the issue.

While one does not want to think about the end of a marriage while thinking about marriage, religion has played a role in divorce as well. Even today, some religions do not allow divorced people to be remarried in the church, and others require religious approval for divorces. The Catholic Church does have divorce, but it only allows the remarriage of a divorced person if the first marriage has been annulled, meaning that the marriage never existed in the first place (and so would not have needed to have a divorce). Some states in the United States were historically very restrictive of divorce, with some requiring the spouse to have been caught in the act of infidelity to allow a divorce. This, in turn, reduced the number of divorces while raising the number of married spouses living apart (and of course the latter does not have statistics kept on it).

An old song (originally done by Buck Fizz (but only released much later) and made famous by Tina Turner) once asked, "What's Love Got to Do with It," but the question here seems to be more one of "What's God got to do with it?" The answer seems to be "everything" for many in terms of same-sex marriage. (Of course, that only considers religions that have a singular God, but the highest religions in the United States (in terms of popularity) almost all have a singular God at the center, even though they use different names.) Same-sex marriage is also one of the few areas where religious belief entered the public sphere, particularly in marriage. No state requires church approval for divorce. Some states make divorce (or marriage) more restrictive than another, but all states respect another state's divorce decree. States have also been ordered to respect other states' adoption decrees.

There are some questions that are not being considered here. Among those are whether religion should affect one's view of other people's same-sex marriage (or of marriage in general). It is not being considered for several reasons, including that religion obviously does affect that view. We are also not considering whether religion should affect one's view of one's own marriage, as that would seem to be very personal and not overly affect public policy. We are also not considering which religion is right. Some people seem to pick up books on religion seeking to find one to validate their religion or to denigrate someone else's. That is not the goal here. The goal is to discuss the rise of marriage equality and how far it has left to go.

This book also does not examine the question of same-sex attraction and whether a religion condemns it. Most religions that ban same-sex marriage (if not all) also condemn same-sex attraction, but that is a topic for a different book. Of course, most religions (if not all) that allow same-sex marriage also accept gay men and women. That is, once again, a topic for another book.

This book is a survey of the tumultuous relationship between same-sex marriage and religion. The *Obergefell* decision made marriage equality the law of the land, and people should respect that. Other books argue for same-sex marriage being allowed for reasons beyond *Obergefell* or for overturning the string of decisions over 10 years (more actually) that led to *Obergefell*. These include works such as Emily Gill's *An Argument for Same-Sex Marriage*, which grounds the right for same-sex marriage in civic equality, which is a step beyond what *Obergefell* says. This book takes *Obergefell* as a given and builds upon it to see how the issue of religion interacts with the topic of allowed same-sex marriage.

Some areas are touched on that do not deal directly with same-sex marriage but more the effects of marriage. That emphasizes what people have said all along: marriage is an important social institution, not just a word, and so if one denies the right to marry, this is an important denial, even when a parallel status might be created with something like a civil union or a domestic partnership.

This book also does not claim to cover all the areas affected by same-sex marriage and religion. No one volume could do that. Nor does it cover all religions. It has been estimated that there are at least 300 religions in the United States (and probably more, as that was based on a survey of only 50,000 people). Now, granted, the survey tried to be accurate, so any percentages given might be right or at least a good approximation; however, there are surely small religions out there, with only a few thousand adherents, that would not hit in a survey that only hit 1 in 6,000 (after all, with only 1,000 adherents, any religion would have a less than 1 in 6 chance to be hit by such a survey).

Thus, while the *Obergefell* decision legalized same-sex marriage across the United States, the issue was not concluded. This book looks at the current state of marriage equality. It also examines what various religions say about same-sex marriage. By fully understanding the diversity of opinion on the issue, along with how the issue has developed over time, the United States (and the world) can decide how to move into the future.

# Acknowledgments

It is said that it takes a village to raise a child. Having not finished with my two yet, I'm not sure if it will take a village or a nation, but it definitely takes a village to help out writing a book. I'd like to thank some of that village but also realize that I will miss some. To the overlooked villager, I apologize.

I'd like to thank the team at ABC-CLIO, as they've been great again. I particularly thank Erin Ryan, who oversaw the final production effort of the book. George Butler took the lead in getting the book started, and numerous other people helped along the way.

I'd also like to thank my family. It's been a long journey writing my three books with ABC-CLIO. Sam, my youngest, was just born when I started writing for ABC-CLIO, and he is now almost ready to enter high school. Caroline was four, and now I am taking her on college visits.

Jessie Powell, my wife, has been my best supporter and my toughest critic. Even more than that, she often took on the tougher job of parenting our two children to release me to work on this book. For all of that, I am eternally grateful.

Many different people in libraries have helped along the way. Troy's library staff was especially helpful.

Any errors that remain, of course, are my own.

# Overview

This book examines the relationship between same-sex marriage and religion in an encyclopedia format. It lists and surveys the top 10 religions in the United States (in terms of size) and sees how their views on same-sex marriage have changed. It also examines some of the most important legal cases. The issue of same-sex marriage is not only a legal one, but in the United States, the changes did come around largely due to the court system. This work includes many of the people who were instrumental in changing the landscape of same-sex marriage and those who were still fighting for equal treatment. It also adds in many additional resources for a further study of the material once this book has been looked at.

Among the cases examined are *Obergefell*, the 2015 case that mandated that all states reflect marriage equality, and *Masterpiece Cakeshop*, the 2018 case that held that a business could refuse to serve same-sex couples based on the business owner's religious beliefs. One might think that this issue is over, as *Obergefell* made marriage equality the law of the land, but not every state wants to follow *Obergefell*; some even find unique ways to avoid it. Religions are also having to deal with the issue, and some religions either have splintered recently or are considering it.

The book also provides a detailed chronology of same-sex marriage and makes it clear how long the issue has been present. Many people assume that this is a relatively new issue, but the timeline indicates that it has been around for thousands of years. Special attention is paid to the 1993 *Baehr v. Miike* case in Hawaii that jump-started the modern debate over same-sex marriage and to the 1996 Defense of Marriage Act (DOMA) that tried to quarantine off those states that did allow marriage equality. In each development, attention is paid to the religious elements.

The legal elements are also heavily emphasized. The reason for this is that the law was what forced the United States to adopt marriage equality. Without the U.S. Supreme Court cases of *Obergefell* and *Windsor* (as well as the many cases that led up to them), there is no way that all states without marriage equality at the time would have adopted it within a short period. Also, without the Hawaii 1993 case, the public would have never considered the issue. Even though there had been an LGBTQ equality movement for nearly 25 years before 1993, no states had moved anywhere near allowing same-sex marriage. Less than 25 years after the 1993 decision, there was marriage equality everywhere in the United States, at least legally, and this proves the important nature of the courts. There were also many litigants who were important. Behind every case was a dedicated force of individuals bringing about marriage equality. While the laws are secular, not religious, and only some of the individuals were religious, they are still important to the history of the issue, as they are the ones that eventually brought about the marriage equality that was celebrated in 2015.

Toward the end of the book, there is also a detailed list of important books to read on the topic. This list is annotated so that one has more than just the title to go on when picking out a book to read on the topic for more information. This allows for further reading and study. This book takes a broad approach to the topic, and so it encourages further reading. In addition to the annotated bibliography, after each entry, there is also a list of further readings that includes the sources used for the entry. Most of the books in both were written within the last 10 years, making the volume up to date. Of course, the recent nature of the topic encourages the sources to be modern as well. Even within that fact, though, a focus on newer books was kept. However, new books and articles are coming out every month on the topic, so there is no way to keep updating the reading list.

Ten religions are considered in terms of how they treat same-sex marriage. In each, it looks both at how same-sex marriage is being treated now and how the topic has been treated in the past 30 years or so. As same-sex marriage was not a large public issue before the 1990s, there is obviously not that much research or discussion on any time period before that. Ten religions were picked rather than some other number to allow for variety and so that other elements could be considered rather than just having a list of religions and their reactions. No book could cover all the religions in the United States without extending to multiple volumes and still excluding everything else. The religions included here are a jumping off point to discuss different religions and their views. One note of caution should be made: the inclusion or exclusion of a religion on the list of the 10 considered is not an endorsement or a condemnation; different lists include different religions. Religions will also shift over time in terms of how popular they are, and so this is just a snapshot of the present.

Many different churches have different stances on same-sex marriage. It is not as simple as most churches support it while others oppose it or that most churches oppose it while some support it. In truth, there are not as many stances on the issue as there are religions, even though sometimes it seems that way. Looking at the 10 most popular religions (by number of adherents), some of those religions, such as the Catholic Church, ban same-sex marriage, while others, such as the Presbyterians, allow it. In some who allow it, like the Presbyterians, each church is given the power to decide on a local level their minister, which in turn allows local control over what level of support to give marriage equality. In still others, such as the Methodist Church, the position is noted to be evolving. The word *noted* is used here to suggest that other religions may also be evolving, but the Methodist Church is currently fighting over it publicly. The position of churches as a whole is also evolving.

Although this book looks a fair amount at the relative present and the future, the history of same-sex marriage is also very important. This is true for two reasons. First, in slowly changing areas, many are resistant to change because, as one might say, "It's always been different." To see how accurate that is, a knowledge of the past is important. (Those quickly changing areas that are new do not have that concern.) If the past was different, we also need to know what the past was and why that was the past. History is often used as a defense of the status quo and has been a reason for resistance to change in regard to same-sex marriage.

Also, changes that come about often aim to correct past wrongs, and so it is important to see how the past changed and evolved and why change has occurred. Very often, change that occurs—and this is very true in same-sex marriage—has evolved for a reason. It also shows whether things were always the same in the past and how long things have been the same as they are now (and when they started changing). The historical material also shows how things quickly changed and heated up in the 2000s. In 2004, John Kerry lost the presidential election in part due to the same-sex marriage issue. He did not advocate for it, but his opponent, George W. Bush, claimed that Kerry supported it. Kerry was then unable to get out of the way of the movement. By the end of the 2000s, a majority of people supported marriage equality.

The U.S. Supreme Court served an important role in the same-sex marriage battle. That body, obviously, was the place that upheld marriage equality for the entire country in the 2015 *Obergefell* decision. The court also took an important step just before that in 2013 with the *Windsor* decision. The Supreme Court changed its view from the *Windsor* case to the *Obergefell* decision, and it changed its view from the 1990s to *Obergefell*. This shows that the Supreme Court's doctrine developed over time.

While one might think that it took a long time for the Supreme Court to act, as it was 20 years from the Hawaii case (at the state supreme court level) to the 2015 *Obergefell* case, the Supreme Court still acted well before the U.S. Congress or many state legislatures. Similar to what happened with school integration, the Supreme Court acted to protect the rights of minorities well before the publicly elected bodies in most areas. This book examines in part how the Supreme Court doctrine changed over time and how the court interacted with other elected bodies.

The *Obergefell* decision also might have seemed to conclude the issue, but it did not. This work also looks at several decisions after the 2015 *Obergefell* decision, including the 2018 *Masterpiece Cakeshop* decision about when discrimination against those in a same-sex marriage is allowed. The *Masterpiece Cakeshop* decision was a step backward for marriage equality, but the principle was affirmed in other decisions, such as *Pavan*. This book looks at all the important Supreme Court decisions of the time period.

While the Supreme Court is often the focus of issues, other courts are important as well. It was, after all, the Hawaii Supreme Court that started the whole marriage equality movement going forward with its ruling in 1993 that three couples could marry in the state (although this decision was later overturned by a constitutional amendment). State courts also led to several states adopting or allowing marriage equality in the decades following. Some state court decisions forced the legislature to act, which means that the legislature was ultimately the one to act, but without the state courts, it is pretty clear that no action would ever have taken place.

The state courts were also important on the national level. The state tribunals might be viewed as part of the prequel to *Windsor* and *Obergefell*, and so they are less emphasized in some accounts. However, without some states doing it first, it is unlikely that the U.S. Supreme Court would have allowed marriage equality to take place in the end. One state needed to be first to get the rest of the nation thinking about it. Here, it was two states: first, Hawaii, which was overturned by a constitutional amendment, and second, Massachusetts, where an attempt at a constitutional amendment banning same-sex marriage failed and the state adopted same-sex marriage.

In many ways, the move toward marriage equality was a true federal effort. The state-level efforts sparked federal change, which in turn caused more state change. By the end, marriage equality became active across the entire country in this way. But the changes did not come to each state equally and definitely not at the same pace. Some states even now have a fair percentage of people who publicly or privately oppose same-sex marriage, and one must keep that in mind when understanding how opinions on same-sex marriage evolved and continued to evolve. This is a different book than one that might have been written 10 years ago.

Based on what has been noted so far, one might think that it has been all large-scale states and federal movements that brought about marriage equality. However, that would be far from the truth. There were a number of groups and movements that were very important in the drive toward same-sex marriage and explaining why it took as long as it did. Some of these groups are noted multiple times. Many of these movements did not arise in 1993 with the first Hawaii court decision but were around long before that. Without those groups already being in place, marriage equality would not have occurred.

Looking at the effect of all these groups shows why the process was as complicated as it became. There were groups promoting it as well as resisting it. Those promoting marriage equality, above and beyond the people suing, show that lawsuits and efforts for equality have developed far from the idea that one person alone can make a difference in politics. They also show the need for organization and working together to get things done.

While there were groups who supported marriage equality, there were also quite a few different groups discussed in this book who opposed it. The groups discussed were part of the reason that it took over two decades to have marriage equality. One must wonder what happened to these groups. Some of the groups, over time, changed their views on the subject. Others, seeing how the wind was blowing, gave in to the inevitable and accepted same-sex marriage.

However, some still remain. Of those that remain, some kept fighting against marriage equality and hoped to get the Supreme Court to reconsider *Obergefell*. Others simply moved to defending other positions and claiming that they had been consistent all along. Some of the last set changed from trying to ban all same-sex marriages to trying to defend the right of some not to serve those in same-sex marriages. This shows that opposition did not go away just because of *Obergefell* and that those who favor marriage equality still need to remain vigilant.

The groups opposed to marriage equality show how resistance shifts over time and how even after a victory is won in the Supreme Court, there are still forces that oppose that victory, similar to what occurred with desegregation.

It was not just a particular group or area that changed, but all of society. In many ways, this book documents how much society differed from the 1960s to now. From the Stonewall riots to *Obergefell* was less than 50 years, but in that time period, LGBTQ individuals moved from being wholly marginalized to being noted as equal by the Supreme Court.

The period that is mostly discussed here, the 20 years from 1995 to 2015, saw equally massive change in the law as well as society. People moved from being mostly against any sort of equal treatment of same-sex unions to mostly favoring marriage equality. That is a huge movement for just a generation. While the law is often discussed, society moved too. Without that societal movement, the nation would have never accepted, even as much as it did, the 2015 *Obergefell* decision.

However, not all of society has moved to favor marriage equality. Some have moved to allowing it in other areas, but not in their area. In other words, a florist might be okay with marriage equality, just as long as they do not have to sell flowers to the couple. Others have allowed it in their minds as long as the couple getting married does not move into their neighborhood or infringe on a person's religious freedom, however that is defined.

This book also shows the importance of marriage. While many in opposite-sex marriages often presented *marriage* as "only a word" when suggesting alternatives to same-sex couples, same-sex couples knew that it was much more than just a word. It clearly gave same-sex couples more equality in society than any other treatment. Marriage is a status that society and the law consider to be very important, and it also affects a large number of other areas. These include adoption, both in the eyes of some states and in the eyes of society and the church, and baptism, as different churches treated those in same-sex marriages differently.

This work also emphasizes the benefits to marriage, which further shows why marriage equality is important. There have been cases where the government has treated those in same-sex marriages different from those in opposite-sex marriages. One example of this is in surrogacy, where the mother and father of a surrogate child (regardless of who donated the sperm and egg) are listed on a birth certificate. However, in the case of a lesbian couple, only one mom would be listed.

One element in common in all these areas is the force of people. People were an important factor in the drive toward marriage equality and a more equal society. This means that the people sometimes need to be considered, even though history is sometimes complained about being one person after another. Pete Buttigieg, the first openly gay presidential candidate, is among the important figures. Without the drive and sacrifice of individuals, change would not have ever come about.

However, individuals also sometimes played an important role in slowing down the drive toward marriage equality, and among those discussed is George W. Bush, who won the 2004 presidential campaign in part by emphasizing his opposition to same-sex marriage and his opponent's (John Kerry) support of it, even though Kerry was lukewarm in his support.

This book examines the whole same-sex marriage debate and recent developments. This sea change from no state having same-sex marriage to every state having it in only 20 years is one of the most rapid in U.S. history. Examining the reasons for this quick change shows that society has largely shifted its view on same-sex marriage. The U.S. Supreme Court also changed its view relatively quickly. However, the issue was also relatively clear, and the arguments in favor of marriage equality were very strong. This explains the rapid shift over a short amount of time. To fully understand it, one must look at society, the legal developments, and the shifts in opinion as all feeding one another. Religion also played a role in the opposition, and religions have shifted over time. People also played a large role, and the prominent personalities must be remembered. However, these decisions were also about the little people who do not often make it into the history books. After all, in the end, the Supreme Court's words mean that people are equal, regardless of whom they love, and that is the end takeaway from all of these debates and discussions.

Same-sex marriage remains a very controversial topic. While those who support it might not consider it such, the very fact that their opponents do not accept marriage equality suggests otherwise. This volume looks at the history, the important legal cases, and the current state of same-sex marriage. The particular focus here is on religion, as religion forms a large portion of the opposition. While not all opposed to same-sex marriage cite religion, that issue is one of the few successful ways that marriage equality has been opposed. On the whole, marriage equality and religion definitely need to be evaluated.

# Chronology

**1000 BCE**—In China, Pan Zhang and Wang Zhongxian's story is recorded, and they are described as having the same relationship as that of husband and wife. No official marriage is recorded though.

**Late Middle Ages**—In France, particularly, legal documents of "brotherment" are used to bind two people of the same gender (very often men) together. In at least some cases, the attraction was a sexual one.

**1700s**—In France, many priests turn down same-sex couples for marriage when one person poses as the man and one as the woman. Some of those couples go to another priest and are married.

**1807**—Charity Bryant and Sylvia Drake start living together publicly as a couple in Vermont. They are one of the first public same-sex couples in American history. They live together for 40 years, until Charity's death.

**19th century**—In the United States, many female couples live in "Boston marriages," where they live together for years and sometimes even own property together. Records indicate that some of these couples were lovers. Others probably found it easier to live in such an arrangement than to have to live at their parents' house, which was often the only other option for single women of that time period.

**1950s**—"Homosexuality" is linked with un-Americanism in the Cold War, and many actions are taken to criminalize gay orientation, including an increased emphasis on banning gay men and women from the military and workforce.

**1953**—*One Magazine* publishes a story on "homosexual marriage." The U.S. Post Office screens it for nearly a month before deciding that it is not obscene.

**1970**—Jack Baker and Mike McConnell apply for a marriage license in Hennepin County, Minnesota. Their application is denied. In late 1971, the Minnesota Supreme Court upholds the denial.

**1971**—Baker and McConnell, in Mankato County, Minnesota, apply for and get a marriage license. They are then married. This is seen by many as the first same-sex marriage in American history, even though some legal courts before 2015 do not treat this as a marriage.

**1973**—Maryland bans same-sex marriage. This is believed to be the first state to directly ban same-sex marriage by statute.

**1976**—Two gay men in Washington State try to get married (without a marriage license) in the Episcopal Church, which turns them down.

**1980**—The Equal Rights Amendment (ERA) is opposed because some churches, including the Mormon Church, believe that it could lead to same-sex marriage. The ERA reads in part, "Equality of rights under the law shall not be denied or abridged by the United States or by any state on account of sex." It was proposed in the 1920s, finalized in this wording in the 1940s, passed by Congress in 1972, and has since failed to win ratification by enough states.

**1982**—AIDS is formally named. Its explosion onto the scene highlights how many more rights opposite-sex partners, in general, and married couples, specifically, have over same-sex couples who cannot marry. In most, if not all cases, distant family members have more rights than the longtime partners of AIDS victims.

**1983**—Rights for same-sex couples are an issue because of the AIDS epidemic. However, the first legal test comes about because of a car accident. Sharon Kowalski and Karen Thompson are a couple when Sharon is hit by a drunk driver. Karen wants control of Sharon's legal and medical decisions but has no legal standing. She sues, and a nearly decade-long legal battle follows.

**1984**—Berkeley passes the first domestic partnership benefits in the country.

**1987**—During the Second National March for Gay and Lesbian Rights in Washington, DC, a wedding is held in which over 3,000 couples are married. As the couples do not have marriage certificates, the marriages are not legal, but it is a symbolic protest and the kickoff in some ways of the march toward marriage equality.

**1989**—New York's highest court holds that a same-sex couple should be considered a family for state regulations. While this might not seem to be controversial, this is the first time that a state supreme court or its equivalent has held that view.

**1990**—Three same-sex couples in Hawaii apply for a marriage license. They are turned down and take the case to the Hawaii Supreme Court.

**1992**—Companies begin to give same-sex partners benefits. One company to do this was Levi's.

**1993**—The Hawaii Supreme Court rules that a state provision forbids the denial of a marriage license based on gender. This was based on a 1990 case. The state provision in question denied discrimination based on sex.

**1995**—Utah signs a Defense of Marriage Act, which states that Utah does not have to recognize a marriage from outside the state. This is probably aimed at Hawaii's pending case over whether Hawaii has to issue marriage certificates to same-sex couples wanting to marry (which Utah would then have to consider whether to recognize). It should be noted that most states recognized marriages from all other states, regardless of who was married.

**1996**—Various states issue proclamations against same-sex marriage. In Alabama, Governor Fob James issues a proclamation saying that no state official would have to recognize an out-of-state same-sex marriage. This is a bit premature, as no state has same-sex marriage and Hawaii's is still going through the appeals process.

In a state trial court, a Hawaii court rules that the state would have to prove a "compelling interest" to restrict the three couples' right to marry (this was an extension of the case that began in 1990). The ruling is halted, as Hawaii was working on a constitutional amendment to ban same-sex marriage. This is the ruling that prompts the Defense of Marriage Act.

As a response to the Hawaii trial court case (and enacted before the trial court's decision), the U.S. Congress passes the Defense of Marriage Act (DOMA). It has two parts. First, no state is required to respect any other state's marriage laws (this is aimed at allowing any other state to not respect a same-sex marriage from Hawaii if one occurs). Second, all federal laws that refer to marriage are talking about one man and one woman.

**1997**—Hawaii, as a sort of compromise, offers domestic partnership benefits, but only for certain companies and for certain benefits. This is somewhat of a triple marriage light—different name, only certain companies, and only certain benefits.

**1998**—Hawaii enacts a state constitutional amendment defining marriage as between one man and one woman, thus overturning the 1996 trial court (which most assumed would have been upheld in the state supreme court had it gotten that far).

An Alaska trial court holds that the state must establish a compelling interest for a ban on same-sex marriage. In a pattern soon to be familiar, Alaska then passes a state constitutional amendment banning same-sex marriage. This provision reverses the court's decision.

**1999**—California adopts a same-sex partnership statute, the first state to do so.

For the first time, a state court (in this case, Vermont) holds that a ban on same-sex marriage violates the Vermont Constitution. Vermont is ordered by the Vermont Supreme Court to either grant gays and lesbians the right to marry or to establish an equivalent alternative.

**2000**—A conference of Reformed Jewish rabbis (rabbis who are in the Reformed branch of Judaism) vote to recognize and sanction marriages and partnerships for same-sex couples. They are the first branch of Judaism to do so.

Vermont adopts civil unions, or what was called by many people "marriage light." As most other states do not have civil unions, the question of whether a same-sex civil union has to be honored by another state is avoided.

California, the largest U.S. state, approves state Proposition 22 by a wide margin, creating a state law that bans same-sex marriage.

**2001**—The Netherlands allows same-sex marriage, the first country to do so.

**2002**—The Federal Marriage Amendment is introduced. It would have created a federal amendment enshrining into the U.S. Constitution the definition of a *marriage* as being between a man and a woman.

**2003**—In Massachusetts, the state supreme court holds that the Massachusetts Constitution requires same-sex marriage to be allowed. This touches off a battle to perhaps amend the constitution to ban same-sex marriage.

New Jersey adopts a same-sex partnership program with a domestic partnership arrangement. It is one of the first states to have a domestic partnership system.

The U.S. Supreme Court strikes down same-sex sodomy laws. This enlarges the idea of sexual privacy and gives both gay and straight people the same privacy rights in this area.

In a relatively belated move, as the Dutch had legalized same-sex marriage two years before, the Vatican begins a large-scale formal effort to get rid of same-sex marriage.

A poll shows that Americans are generally opposed to allowing same-sex couples to marry.

California extends benefits to same-sex partners. It is one of the first large states to do this.

**2004**—The king of Cambodia announces support for same-sex marriage. He is one of the first heads of state to do so. Cambodia is also one of the first countries outside of Europe to do so.

Massachusetts allows same-sex couples to be married, becoming the first state to allow the occurrence.

George W. Bush fails in his effort to get Congress to pass the Federal Marriage Amendment. The majority voted for it in the House (but still about 47 votes short of the two-thirds needed), and the Senate voted 49 to 48 to end debate (but 60 votes were needed to end debate, and 67 were needed for ratification). The amendment thus falls far short in both the House and Senate.

Maine adds domestic partnerships as it becomes the latest state to adopt a "marriage-light" proposal. It does require any domestic partners to have lived in the state for the past 12 months.

A town in New York, New Paltz, starts issuing marriage licenses to same-sex couples. This is part of the efforts by those favoring marriage equality to force the issue.

George W. Bush handily defeats John Kerry in the presidential election. He not only wins the Electoral College, but he is also the only Republican to win the popular vote in over 30 years (1989–present). Kerry's perceived support of same-sex marriage is a major issue that lost him support.

On one day (Election Day 2004), 11 states pass constitutional amendments banning same-sex marriage. This is, in many ways, the highwater mark for opponents of marriage equality.

A new national poll suggests that a majority of Americans favor civil unions and states making their own policies. However, most Americans do not yet favor a nationwide allowance of same-sex marriage.

San Francisco, California, performs same-sex weddings in a direct violation of California's law. The city is eventually forced to cease the practice.

England moves to allow spousal benefits to same-sex couples, joining a movement spreading across Europe. This allows gays and lesbians in England to have many of the same legal benefits, such as joint insurance, as opposite-sex couples. However, England does not yet move to allow same-sex marriage.

California overturns marriages that occurred for a while in the state, thus voiding about 4,000 same-sex marriages that had occurred.

**2005**—Pope John Paul II speaks out against same-sex marriage, continuing the Vatican's strong stance against it.

New York rules that a ban on same-sex marriage is illegal. It is the first large state to do so.

Kansas takes a stance against same-sex marriage by a wide margin. This continues the split in the country, where the middle takes a strong stance against same-sex marriage while the coasts move toward allowing it.

A California state judge rules the 2000 law limiting marriage to a man and a woman is a violation of the equal protection clause. Tradition, in the judge's mind, is not enough to justify this constitutional violation.

Connecticut approves civil unions, becoming the second state to do so. It does this by passing a bill in the state house and senate. It is the first state to do so via legislation.

California passes a same-sex marriage law, but the governor vetoes the law, in part because the voters had created the state ban in 2000 with Proposition 22. The governor believes that the voters should have the final say. There are not enough legislators who favor the bill to override the veto.

The United Church of Christ allows same-sex marriages. It is one of the first large Christian denominations to take this stance.

Canada allows same-sex marriage. This brings same-sex marriage right to the literal border of the United States.

Nebraska's ban on same-sex marriage is struck down by a federal court. This is one of the first victories for marriage equality in the federal courts.

**2006**—Nebraska's same-sex marriage ban is reinstated by a federal appeals court. The reasoning given was that limiting marriage to a man and a woman was rationally related to a legitimate state interest, as required, and so would be allowed. This line of ruling would soon fall by the wayside. The federal appeals court ruling was not appealed to the U.S. Supreme Court.

New Jersey is ordered by its supreme court to recognize same-sex unions. The domestic partnerships it had previously allowed are held to not be enough. The court gives the legislature six months to either adopt civil unions or allow same-sex marriage. In late 2006, New Jersey adopts civil unions.

South Africa allows same-sex marriage. It is one of the first states on the African continent to do so, and it does so despite opposition from the Zulus, one of the largest tribes.

Alabama bans same-sex marriage in a constitutional amendment. A sign of Alabama's opposition is that 81 percent of the people vote to approve the amendment.

**2007**—New Jersey adds civil unions in a bow to its state supreme court, which in 2006 had ordered the state to add either civil unions or same-sex marriage. This follows the pattern of mostly the coastal states allowing same-sex marriage or civil unions (by this point, there were six places with civil unions and one with marriage). Vermont is the one lone noncoastal state.

Washington State adds domestic partnerships.

**2008**—The Coquille Native American tribe allows same-sex marriage. While the tribal reservation is entirely in Oregon, the federal government allows Native American tribes to make their own religious and own marriage laws. By 2008, the Cherokee and Navajo had voted to ban same-sex marriage, but most tribes were silent on the issue as of 2008.

The California Supreme Court overturns the state law banning same-sex marriage. This leads to Proposition 8, an amendment to the California State Constitution banning same-sex marriage. California was not the only state to approve a constitutional amendment at this time; Florida and Arizona did the same thing.

The Connecticut Supreme Court orders the state to allow same-sex marriage. Connecticut joins Massachusetts as the only other state to allow same-sex marriage. (California was in the process of deciding what it wanted to do.) Connecticut was also the first state court to hold that civil unions were not enough (Connecticut had tried those in place of marriage) to provide equal protection to all who wanted to marry.

**2009**—The Iowa Supreme Court declares the ban on same-sex marriage that the state had passed to be unconstitutional. This is seen as important because it is the first state in the middle of the country to do this (the others being on the East Coast). Also, there is no residency requirement, so anyone can come in from another state and get married, doubly making this more of a national issue than it had been. In the same year, Maine and New Hampshire both legalize same-sex marriage through the legislature.

Washington, DC, legalizes same-sex marriage, taking a stand in a federally regulated space (Congress somewhat regulates DC as opposed to it having statehood) opposite DOMA, which denied marriage equality.

The California Supreme Court upholds Proposition 8. However, the court also reminds California that sexual orientation is protected by the state constitution at the same level as race and gender, making discrimination on any of those grounds (when found) to be generally illegal.

Vermont legalizes same-sex marriage, joining nearby neighbors Connecticut and Massachusetts.

Maine votes against same-sex marriage, reversing the state legislature. This is one of the few cases where a state legislature legalized same-sex marriage and the voters reversed it (the other is California). Where marriage was legalized and then banned, the process was generally a court decision that was then reversed by a state constitutional amendment.

Wisconsin allows domestic partnerships. This is the second state in the middle of the country to do so. This shows that tolerance of measures near to marriage, even if not fully equal, is starting to spread into the middle of the country.

2010—Washington, DC, starts same-sex marriage, and long lines gather at the courthouse, showing that many people want to participate.

Iceland becomes the first nation with an openly gay and married leader when the prime minister marries her partner.

Argentina legalizes same-sex marriage. It is the first South American country to do so.

Proposition 8 is declared unconstitutional, and California declines to defend it. However, another group steps in to defend it, causing the court battle to continue.

New Hampshire adopts same-sex marriage. This means that every state in New England, other than Maine, has adopted marriage equality.

"Don't Ask, Don't Tell" is repealed, meaning that gay men and women can openly serve in the military. This repeal ends a nearly 20-year public battle on the issue and a quieter private war running back into the 1950s at least.

2011—President Obama declines to defend DOMA, even though it is a federal law. A group of Republican congressmen organize to defend the law.

New York adopts same-sex marriage. New York is the largest state to do so thus far, other than when California did for a short period.

President Obama pushes a bill to repeal DOMA, although this does not come to pass.

Illinois adopts civil unions, meaning that several of the larger states have taken a step toward marriage equality.

2012—Proposition 8 is declared illegal by a federal appeals court, as those favoring it had appealed the 2011 decision at the federal district court holding it unconstitutional.

Hawaii adopts civil unions. This in many ways moves the issue almost full circle, as Hawaii's courts (in 1993) first allowed same-sex marriages and then the voters overturned it.

North Carolina adds a ban on same-sex marriage to its constitution. It is one of the last states to take this step.

President Obama comes out fully in defense of same-sex marriage. As he had favored the repeal of DOMA, this is somewhat anticlimactic but still important, as he is the first president to do so. In many ways, this shows how far the United States had come since 2004, when John Kerry's muted stand on gay marriage (he refused to fully condemn it while George W. Bush called for a constitutional amendment banning it) cost Kerry the presidency. Now, in 2012, Obama defends gay marriage and still wins the presidency.

An appeals court rules against DOMA, and this sets up the U.S. Supreme Court for a ruling on the issue.

Maine, Maryland, and Washington State legalize same-sex marriage by voter initiative. They are some of the earlier states to do this, as most other states had only done so as a result of the courts or the legislature.

**2013**—Rhode Island approves same-sex marriage in the legislature. This is significant in part due to the heavily Roman Catholic nature of Rhode Island (the church still opposes same-sex marriage) and because this means double digits of states favor same-sex marriage.

Delaware approves same-sex marriage, another state on the coast. This is significant because it happens only a year after Delaware started doing civil unions, showing how rapidly things are changing.

Colorado approves civil unions. This means that yet another state in the middle of the country has taken a step toward marriage equality.

The federal government allows same-sex partners to have some marriage benefits. This is a great shift from the 1990s, when lesbians and gays were hounded out of the military directly, and even the 2000s, when "Don't Ask, Don't Tell" created confusion in the military and drove many gays and lesbians out.

Minnesota legalizes same-sex marriage. This is the 12th state to do so, and, more significantly, it is the second state in the middle of the country to do so.

*United States v. Windsor* finds DOMA to be unconstitutional as it applies to the federal government. In this case, the federal government was required to treat same-sex marriages the same as opposite-sex marriages (in this case, it was dealing with inheritance taxes).

In *Hollingsworth v. Perry,* California's Proposition 8 is upheld on the grounds that those trying to defend it lacked standing (when California was not willing to defend it, a private group stepped in).

California resumes same-sex marriage. It had been put on hold, obviously, while the *Hollingworth v. Perry* (Proposition 8) case made its way to the U.S. Supreme Court.

The IRS recognizes same-sex couples. This was largely expected in light of the *United States v. Windsor* decision earlier in the year.

Illinois recognizes same-sex marriage. Three of the largest states (New York, Illinois, and California) are now standing up for marriage equality, and Illinois is the largest state in the middle of country holding in favor of it. Three of the largest five have now legalized it; Florida and Texas are still resistant to the efforts.

New Jersey starts allowing same-sex marriage. Governor Christie, a Republican, acknowledges defeat and says that the state will stop opposing efforts to have marriage equality. This means that all the coastal states north of Virginia (and all the West Coast states other than Oregon) have marriage equality.

A federal judge strikes down Utah's same-sex marriage ban. This shows that even in the most conservative areas of the United States, a same-sex marriage ban may not survive.

New Mexico allows same-sex marriage due to a state supreme court ruling. New Mexico was somewhat unique in that no laws or constitutional provisions ruled on the subject. It was the only state to neither have a state constitutional amendment nor a state law allowing or banning it (as of 2013). However, state laws and practices had generally worked to prevent same-sex marriage. New Mexico was also somewhat unique because the decision came about due to county clerks asking the state supreme court for guidance in an unclear area; it was one of the few that came about in this way.

Hawaii allows same-sex marriage. This is the fifteenth state, which is important because it only took less than a year to get from 10 (Rhode Island) to 15. It is also important because it shows how Hawaii came full circle from being the first state to consider and then ban same-sex marriage before finally allowing it.

2014—The U.S. Supreme Court stops same-sex marriage in Utah by suspending enforcement of the 2013 order overturning Utah's ban.

Nigeria bans same-sex marriage (and also criminalizes a variety of same-sex practices). This proves that marriage equality, and equality in general, is not spreading throughout the entire world.

Pennsylvania declines to challenge a court ruling overturning its ban on same-sex marriage. This means that 19 out of 50 states, or over one-third of the states, now favor marriage equality.

The United Nations recognizes the marriage status of all its employees married in same-sex weddings. This is much broader than its earlier idea, which only recognized the same-sex marriages of those who were from places where same-sex marriage was legal. This greatly increases the number of same-sex spouses who are eligible for benefits.

North Carolina's attorney general declines to defend the state's marriage ban. A ban in Virginia that was similar to one in North Carolina had been struck down. Virginia, though, continued to defend its ban.

The Presbyterian Church, one of the three largest Protestant churches in the United States, votes to allow same-sex marriage ceremonies.

A federal district judge in Oklahoma strikes down Oklahoma's same-sex marriage ban. This was typical of the period as the rulings favoring marriage equality mounted. Also typical was the judge's ruling that marriages had to wait while the decision was appealed. So it was a victory for marriage equality, but the effect was delayed.

Congress refuses to pass a Veterans Administration (VA) benefit extension to all same-sex couples. As of 2014, the benefits were only given where state law allowed same-sex marriages. Some in Congress tried to extend the benefits, but their efforts failed.

A federal district court judge in Tennessee rules that the state must recognize marriages from other states. This is a ruling limited to three specific marriages, but it is pretty much the writing on the wall for Tennessee and other holdouts about marriages from other states.

The U.S. Supreme Court refuses to hear appeals from five states (Indiana, Oklahoma, Utah, Virginia, and Wisconsin), which makes same-sex legal there. This raises the number of states with marriage equality to 24.

Three circuit courts of appeal rule in favor of marriage equality, making same-sex marriage legal in more of the land. However, the Sixth Circuit Court of Appeals, covering Michigan, Ohio, Kentucky, and

Tennessee, rules against marriage equality, effectively guaranteeing that the U.S. Supreme Court will take up the issue in short order. Differences in rulings on the same issue by different circuits greatly increase the chance that the Supreme Court will rule on that issue.

A ruling from Nevada forcing marriage equality is allowed to stand, meaning that a full 26 states (and DC) allow same-sex marriage and 22 have banned it constitutionally. No states, as of October 2014, have civil unions or domestic partnerships or such "marriage-light" arrangements.

Alaska's ban on same-sex marriage is struck down. This is the oldest constitutional ban in the United States, having been passed in 1998.

Idaho's same-sex marriage ban is struck down. However, unlike some other governors, Idaho's governor vows to fight on, and, in an interesting twist, he argues that the overturning of the state law will lessen interest in politics because people will fear that state laws will be struck down. It is unclear whether any data analysis has been done on state voting interest in Idaho since 2014.

Arizona's ban on same-sex weddings is struck down. Unlike Idaho, Arizona's attorney general states that he will not continue the battle.

**2015**—In Florida, same-sex couples are allowed to marry after a district court strikes down the state's same-sex marriage ban. This means that four of the five most populous states now have marriage equality (the lone holdout is Texas).

In January, the U.S. Supreme Court announces that it will hear an appeal of a Sixth Circuit Court of Appeals ruling denying marriage equality in the four states under the Sixth Circuit (Michigan, Ohio, Kentucky, and Tennessee).

In January, Alabama's marriage ban falls. The case was not two people seeking to be married but two people who had been married in California, who had lived together for a decade, who were seeking recognition of their California marriage by the Alabama courts.

In February, couples in Alabama start marrying as the order resulting from the January decision is implemented.

In February, a single couple is married in Texas. Texas allows this marriage, as one of the partners has cancer, but holds firm against any other marriages.

In March, Alabama ceases same-sex marriages after the Alabama Supreme Court orders clerks of the courts to stop issuing marriage licenses.

In April, the U.S. Supreme Court hears arguments in *Obergefell v. Hodges*, which deals with same-sex marriage.

The prime minister of Luxemburg marries his partner. This is the first same-sex marriage of a leader of the European Union (EU).

Ireland votes to allow same-sex marriage. This is somewhat shocking because Ireland is predominantly Catholic, and the Catholic Church still opposes same-sex marriage.

The Episcopal Church votes to allow same-sex weddings. This means that another large Protestant body (the Episcopal Church represents about 1% of the population) now allows same-sex marriage, joining the Presbyterians and Lutherans.

The U.S. Supreme Court, in *Obergefell*, makes same-sex marriage legal in all of the United States and its territories, other than American Samoa and Native American reservations. It is legal on some reservations, but that is up to the tribe. It is still banned in American Samoa.

The Fifth Circuit Court of Appeals orders Louisiana, Mississippi, and Texas to allow marriage equality because of *Obergefell*.

Alabama is ordered by the federal court to allow same-sex marriages because of *Obergefell*.

Attorneys general in some 15 states ask that religious groups be allowed to oppose marriage equality, in opposition to *Obergefell*, but still keep their tax exemptions. This eventually becomes the stance of the Trump administration.

2016—China continues its ban on same-sex marriage, holding against several couples who wanted to marry.

2017—Bermuda ends its same-sex marriages, deciding to have domestic partnerships instead.

2018—An EU court rules that an EU country must recognize a same-sex marriage, even if the country in question does not allow for same-sex marriage.

2019—Taiwan recognizes same-sex marriage. By doing so, it is the first area in Asia to allow same-sex marriage. Asia and Africa remain more resistant to same-sex marriage than the rest of the world.

Ecuador recognizes same-sex marriage. This means that more of South America is recognizing same-sex marriage.

**2020**—The Methodist Church, an international body, seems to be ready to split over the issue of whether to allow same-sex marriage. The group retaining the name will probably allow same-sex marriage ceremonies (the coronavirus delayed the vote scheduled for May 2020). The vote seems pretty clear to cause the split; the only question is when the vote will occur.

A

## Adoption

In many people's minds, the issue of adoption is currently tied to same-sex marriage. However, the two are somewhat unconnected. The history of adoption shows that allowing same-sex couples to marry removes a barrier to adoption. However, other barriers remain. Adoption agencies also had to consider whether to allow same-sex couples to adopt when the sponsoring agency that handled the adoptions was run by a religious organization that opposed same-sex marriage.

Historically, adoption has been seen by many as a way for people to parent who are unable to have children of their own biologically. However, that is not a wholly accurate view. Wealthy people have often adopted, even when they already had biological children. Some wealthy people in history also adopted children, as this made inheritance easier or even legal, as some places did not allow you to leave money to someone who was not your child.

In the United States, adoption changed to a way to place orphaned and homeless children. Orphanages could not handle the need, and so orphan trains were organized, with children given to anyone who would take them in the American West, with the recipient family viewing the orphan as cheap labor. These trains had largely ended by the 1930s. Most sponsoring agencies have long been church affiliated, and states have always been interested in passing off work to charity organizations, if for no other reason than to save money.

By the 20th century, there was the idea of foster care. Over time, as fewer couples who were childless desired children and technology improved for fixing conception issues, other alternatives were considered. Single people were eventually generally allowed to adopt again (rich single people had been able to adopt for a long time), and the issue then

1

became one of whether to allow gay men and women to legally adopt. It should be noted that this entry is only talking about legally allowed adoptions. Many people were raised by relatives or had someone in the community take them in without any formal acknowledgment of the process.

Historically, single people were largely allowed to adopt in most states, even though it was less publicized. It is also generally difficult to find statistics, as throughout most of American history this data was not collected. After World War II, the focus for agencies came to be placing adopted children with what they viewed as normal families, like the Cleavers of *Leave It to Beaver*. This led to public emphasis on the *married* part. However, there were sometimes pushes that encouraged single people to adopt. For gay men and women, the prospect of a home study (and society's general frowning on LGBTQ people) probably discouraged some. Even today, the issue of LGBTQ adoption is not highlighted, with some online histories not including that term (or any similar one) in their index. There are also a lot of areas that still need research. "Much remains to be learned about how discrimination, social norms, and related concepts may affect parenting intentions among lesbian and gay adults" (Tate, Patterson, and Levy 2019, 201).

For statistical reasons, it is difficult to tell the prevalence of LGBTQ adoptions. Such adoptions did happen though. However, many of those adoptions had to be by just one person. In some states, same-sex couples could foster children but not adopt them. "Marriage was never an option for same-sex couples in North Carolina, but prior to 2009 gay [men] and lesbians were allowed to jointly foster children in North Carolina. Those parents were not allowed to jointly adopt the children they fostered. One parent became a legal stranger to their child at the time of adoption" (Maxwell and Kelsey 2014, 261). This would tend to both discourage adoption and make it difficult to do research in this area.

Oddly enough, the situation has almost reversed in one way. Originally, the bias was against single parents for a variety of reasons. Many LGBTQ individuals felt that they were doubly prejudiced: they could not marry, and they were also suffering the consequences of homophobia. Now that they could marry in the 2010s, they were subject to more prejudice, as they were being banned by many church-affiliated adoption agencies. Some of those agencies had undoubtedly placed children with LGBTQ individuals in the past and so now seemed to be saying that it was okay to be gay or lesbian, just do not publicize it or get married. These adoption agencies defended their policy by saying that they did not support same-sex marriage for religious reasons and so should not be forced to go against their religious beliefs.

From a religious perspective, very little was discussed about the needs of the child. No one offered a religious analysis for when the desire to move a child out of foster care outweighed the religion's ban on same-sex marriage. These bans were generally allowed in state courts, and some states wrote exemptions into their adoption policies. Only one state, Michigan (whose policies are discussed in a different entry), forced religious adoption agencies to allow same-sex married couples to adopt without bias.

***See also:*** *Baker v. Nelson*; *Dumont v. Gordon*; Surrogacy; 2000s, The

## Further Reading

Brodzinsky, David, and Adam Pertman. (2012). *Adoption by Lesbians and Gay Men: A New Dimension in Family Diversity*. New York: Oxford University Press.

Conn, Peter J. (2013). *Adoption: A Brief Social and Cultural History*. Palgrave Pivot. New York: Palgrave Macmillan.

Maxwell, Mark Edward, and Gary Kelsey. (2014). "Second Parent Adoption: Same-Sex and the Best Interest of the Child." *Journal of Health and Human Services Administration* 37 (2): 260.

Pierceson, Jason, Adriana Piatti-Crocker, and Shawn Schulenberg. (2010). *Same-Sex Marriage in the Americas: Policy Innovation for Same-Sex Relationships*. Lanham, MD: Lexington Books.

Tate, Doyle P., Charlotte J. Patterson, and Andrew J. Levy. (2019). "Predictors of Parenting Intentions among Childless Lesbian, Gay, and Heterosexual Adults." *Journal of Family Psychology* 33 (2): 194–202.

Working with Lesbian, Gay, Bisexual, Transgender, and Questioning (LGBTQ) Families in Foster Care and Adoption. (2016). *Bulletin for Professionals*. Washington, DC: Child Welfare Information Gateway, Children's Bureau/ ACYF/ACF/HHS.

# AIDS

It may seem odd to have a deadly disease related to marriage equality, but in many ways, and for people on both sides of the marriage equality issue, the AIDS battles were a preview of those to come over same-sex marriage.

By the end of the 1970s, gay people were recognized in the United States, but their public expression was limited to a few areas. In San Francisco and New York City, those wanting tolerance had some political power, but that was about it. The first congressman who was open about his sexuality did so in 1983. The 1970s also saw the rise of vocal opposition to equal treatment. Among these efforts was the battle in Florida over a Miami ordinance that banned discrimination, which was passed and then repealed. However, this all paled in comparison to the AIDS issue.

In 1981, AIDS burst onto the American scene. Americans were terrified of the disease, which many at the time labeled a "gay disease." Some on the right, including the Moral Majority, blamed gay men in general for the disease, and they also suggested that people did not need to help end the plague, which they viewed as coming from God. In many areas, gay men and lesbians had been enjoying more freedom and had not felt the need to mobilize nationally, but clearly such a move was needed to force action on AIDS. Those whose partners had AIDS came to realize that there were many legal barriers to those who were in love with, but not married to, their ill partners. Many LGBTQ activists came of age, so to speak, in these battles, which eventually forced the federal government to fund research into AIDS.

The AIDS fight saw the creation of several organizations that would carry over into the fight for same-sex marriage. Before AIDS, there were few nationwide advocacy groups. However, in 1987, the AIDS Coalition to Unleash Power (ACT UP) formed, and its members began figuring out how to create political pressure and change policies. "ACT UP empowered people living with HIV/AIDS and challenged homophobia, racism and sexism, and other inequalities fueling the AIDS crisis. In the process, the organization ignited gay and lesbian pride, cultivating queer identities and political action" (Stockdill 2018, 48). Lamba Legal had formed in 1973 but now became more visible in this area. Special interest groups also formed. These groups would all be important for the same-sex marriage fight.

The success on the part of those who favored inclusivity also led to other battles and the formation of nationwide networks. Among the next battles were the rights of gay men and lesbians to openly serve in the U.S. military. At first, the U.S. military wished to ban gay individuals, but by the mid-1990s, a policy of "Don't Ask, Don't Tell" (DADT) was adopted, which was not much of a victory for gay service members. While the policy allowed gay individuals to serve, it required them to keep their sexuality private. In short, gay and lesbian service personnel had to hide their personal lives. Those fully opposed to this policy saw it as another attempt by those favoring rights for gay people to push their agenda into the American mainstream. The DADT fight was also one in which those favoring equality had to convince Congress about a policy that would benefit, in many people's minds, only LGBTQ individuals, unlike the earlier fight over AIDS funding, which helped end a disease that targeted everyone.

In addition to national groups, many gay people had started to move more into the national mainstream. As noted, it was the 1980s when politicians first became open about their sexual orientation and some politicians were reelected after "coming out" as gay, which encouraged others to do it. For those who may be thinking that it was not a big deal, it should be noted that most professional male sports leagues still do not have an active, openly gay player in them. By the 1990s, the increased visibility had forced many in United States to start to think about the issue.

This history formed the background for the battle over same-sex marriage. Those battles are covered elsewhere, but the ties between the battle over AIDS and DADT and same-sex marriage need to be emphasized here. Lambda Legal was one of the larger groups supporting some of the early test cases. One might wonder why individuals cannot just fight their own battles. Well, court cases are very expensive. In today's world, it takes years and many hundreds of thousands of dollars to fight a case all the way to the U.S. Supreme Court, and the only groups (other than state and federal governments) who can afford to do this are corporations and advocacy organizations, for the most part. Lambda Legal was already established and had had time to train attorneys and decide its own policy. People had also thought long and hard about the issue, which made them willing to come forward. The AIDS fight had been a large part of this. Without those fights and those organizations, it is less likely that the same-sex marriage fight would have started or eventually been so successful.

*See also:* Chalcedon Movement; Generational Differences; Sodom and Gomorrah; 2000s, The

## Further Reading

Edwards, Lorece V., Shalon M. Irving, and Anita S. Hawkins. (2011). "Till Death Do Us Part: Lived Experiences of HIV-Positive Married African American Women." *Qualitative Report* 16 (5): 1361–1379.

Green, Edward C., and Allison Herling Ruark. (2011). *AIDS, Behavior, and Culture: Understanding Evidence-Based Prevention*. Walnut Creek, CA: Left Coast Press.

Halkitis, Perry N. (2012). "Obama, Marriage Equality, and the Health of Gay Men." *American Journal of Public Health* 102 (9): 1628–1629.

Halkitis, Perry N. (2014). *The AIDS Generation: Stories of Survival and Resilience*. New York: Oxford University Press.

Petro, Anthony Michael. (2015). *After the Wrath of God: AIDS, Sexuality, and American Religion*. New York: Oxford University Press.

Sangaramoorthy, Thurka. (2014). *Treating AIDS: Politics of Difference, Paradox of Prevention*. New Brunswick, NJ: Rutgers University Press.

Stockdill, Brett Cameron. (2018). "Love in the Time of ACT UP: Reflections on AIDS Activism, Queer Family, and Desire." *QED: A Journal in GLBTQ Worldmaking* 5 (1): 48–83.

# B

## *Baehr v. Miike*

In many ways, the *Baehr v. Miike* case* kicked off the modern debate over same-sex marriage. Ninia Baehr and Genora Dancel and two other couples sued the Hawaii State Department of Health, arguing that the state's denial of their marriage application violated the Hawaii Constitution. There had been efforts before, but this was the first one to have a victory at the state level.

The case was filed under the state constitution, which gave more rights than the federal constitution, and it granted a right to privacy. The case was also filed by a local attorney, as no national group would get involved. Lambda Legal, the main national LGBTQ group, also declined; it was still trying to decide how important marriage was and whether such lawsuits were a good use of resources.

The lawsuit lost at the trial court but was appealed to the state supreme court. In 1993, it held that the denial might be a violation of the equal protection clause, even though the court held that the right to privacy was not violated and that the right to marry a same-sex partner is not a fundamental right. The case was then sent back down to the trial court. In 1996, the judge there, Judge Chang, held that the state did not meet its burden of advancing a compelling interest (required to restrict one's rights if the equal protection clause is violated), nor had it proven to use the least restrictive means (also required). Religion did not play a significant role in the ruling. Thus, the state lost on both prongs of the equal protection test.

In between the state supreme court ruling and the trial, the issue had exploded on the state and national levels. On the state level, two different

---

* This case was originally named *Baehr v. Lewin* and is sometimes referred to as such in writings that occurred contemporaneously with the case.

commissions tried to find some level of compromise that would somewhat satisfy public opinion and fully satisfy the constitutional issue. The second commission recommended allowing same-sex marriage, but it was not acted on. On the national level, Congress passed the Defense of Marriage Act (DOMA), to prevent any other state from having to recognize a same-sex marriage from Hawaii. However, this was an important first step. Sant'Ambrogio and Law argued, "On balance, *Baehr* was an important step forward for lesbian, gay, bisexual, and transgender (LGBT) rights and gender equality. By asking the State to explain why same-sex couples could not be married, the Hawai'i Supreme Court opened a dialogue that continues to this day" (2010, 705).

The case continued moving slowly on the legal stage. Judge Chang did not implement his ruling because it would have been impossible to undo marriages that had taken place if the state supreme court reversed him. He may have also been reading the papers, as the next thing that happened in Hawaii was political. In 1998, Hawaii adopted a same-sex marriage ban into its state constitution, which effectively rendered the issue moot. In 1999, the state supreme court recognized exactly that and directed the trial court to rule for the state director of the Hawaii Department of Health. It was around this same time that other states started granting civil unions. "In the 1999 case *Baker v. State*, the Supreme Court of Vermont came closer than any court at that time to granting same-sex couples the right to marry. . . . In response to the court's ruling the Vermont legislature passed a bill creating civil unions for same-sex couples in early 2000" ("Legal Recognition of Same-Sex Relationships" 2009, 757).

Hawaii continued to debate what it should do, and there were multiple forces at work. Some favored marriage equality, some opposed it, and still others were willing to accept a compromise of some sort that would grant at least some of the benefits of marriage for same-sex couples without the title. Even those favoring some action were split, as some thought the legislature should accomplish this and others wanted (or thought it right to have) a state referendum. Of course, one cannot tell whether a state referendum was favored because the proponent of it thought it would turn out the way they wanted in a legal argument for a political end. In 2009, the state passed a civil union bill only to have it vetoed by the governor, who wanted a referendum. In 2011, the state again passed and a new governor signed the civil union bill, and in 2013, Hawaii passed a bill allowing same-sex marriage. Of course, religion was a factor in these debates.

Nationally, the *Baehr* decision kicked off the debate that ended in DOMA, as noted, but it did not end there. Once the discussion was started, it continued to evolve. Some states started banning any recognition of same-sex marriage, while others allowed for civil unions. In 2004, Massachusetts became the first state to allow same-sex marriage— 11 years after *Baehr*—and after that, the discussion accelerated. Finally, in 2015, another 11 years later, with *Obergefell* decision, the nation adopted marriage equality nationwide. Thus, it took as long to get from Hawaii's decision to the first state adopting it as it did from the first state to nationwide.

*See also:* Defense of Marriage Act, The; *Obergefell v. Hodges*; 2004 Elections and Religion; 2000s, The

## Further Reading

Amar, Akhil Reed. (2018). *The Constitution Today: Timeless Lessons for the Issues of Our Era*. New York: Basic Books.

Ball, Carlos A. (2016). *After Marriage Equality: The Future of LGBT Rights*. New York: New York University Press.

Gibson, Rhonda. (2018). *Same-Sex Marriage and Social Media: How Online Networks Accelerated the Marriage Equality Movement*. New York: Routledge, Taylor & Francis Group.

Gill, Emily R. (2012). *An Argument for Same-Sex Marriage: Religious Freedom, Sexual Freedom, and Public Expressions of Civic Equality. Religion and Politics Series*. Washington, DC: Georgetown University Press.

"Legal Recognition of Same-Sex Relationships." (2009). *Georgetown Journal of Gender & the Law* 10 (2): 751–800.

Miller, Debra A. (2012). *Gay Marriage*. At Issue. Farmington Hills, MI: Greenhaven Press.

Sant'Ambrogio, Michael D., and Sylvia A. Law. (2010). "*Baehr v. Lewin* and the Long Road to Marriage Equality." *University of Hawai'i Law Review* 33 (2): 705.

# Baker v. Nelson

Many people first heard about same-sex marriage with the Hawaii Supreme Court decision in 1993. Some might generalize from that and assume that it was the first time that anyone had filed a lawsuit to force marriage equality; however, that would not be accurate.

At least one couple had filed as early as 1970. That couple was Richard Baker and James McConnell in Minnesota. Baker was a law student, and McConnell was a librarian. They had applied for a marriage license and were denied. They then filed in district court. Among other things, they argued that because Minnesota's marriage laws did not specify a man and a woman, it was not required, and reading it as a requirement would violate the U.S. Constitution. Even though the case was in a Minnesota court, many of Baker and McConnell's arguments were based in the U.S. Constitution. Nelson was the clerk of the district court and so was the one sued.

Baker lost at the trial court level and then appealed to the Minnesota Supreme Court. One must wonder how much the case was already decided before arguments were heard, as no justices asked any questions of either Baker's attorney or the attorney for the county. The court then issued a three-page opinion (which is short for judicial opinions) addressing Baker's argument. The court agreed that the Minnesota statute did not specifically state that marriage was between a man and a woman, but it held that the statute "does not authorize marriage between persons of the same sex and that such marriages are accordingly prohibited" (*Baker v. Nelson* 1971).

Minnesota then turned to Baker's claims about the U.S. Constitution. The court held that the only way the U.S. Constitution could have been violated was if the right to marry one's same-sex partner was a fundamental right. The court held that it was not and used a religious justification: "The institution of marriage as a union of man and woman, uniquely involving the procreation and rearing of children within a family, is as old as the book of Genesis" (*Baker v. Nelson* 1971, 186). Thus, religion was a factor in the decision. The court also looked at the *Griswold* case, involving privacy and the right to use contraceptives, and held that the case only applied in the area of a traditional marriage. The fact that marriage had never been limited to only those who could conceive or were of a child-bearing age was apparently either lost on the court or overlooked. The *Griswold* decision had been noted at the time to be very traditional.

Baker then appealed his case to the U.S. Supreme Court, but he lost there as well. The court's opinion was one sentence: "The appeal is dismissed for want of a substantial federal question" (*Baker v. Nelson* 1972). While this proved to be inaccurate over time, it shows the thinking of the

U.S. population, the government, and the Supreme Court in 1972. However, the issue was obviously not over. Some people had noticed the case at the time, even though it was largely forgotten. It was covered on TV by shows like *The Phil Donahue Show*, but few thought it would lead to anything.

Baker and McConnell obtained a marriage license in another country in the period between the district court's decision and the Minnesota Supreme Court's decision and then married in a United Methodist Church. They then presented themselves as married. However, in order to be united, McConnell had to adopt Baker, and he had that decision upheld, as adoption had no age limit. That would seem to suggest that the marriage had no standing in the eyes of the court, as did a ruling in the 2000s that determined Baker and McConnell could not file taxes as married. The reason why this matters is because of the debate over whether Baker and McConnell had the first same-sex marriage in the United States. Some have argued that they did, but the fact that no court seems to have legally recognized it suggests otherwise as far as the law is concerned. Thus, while the two may have filed the first same-sex marriage certificate, they did not, for all practical purposes, have the first legal same-sex marriage. This is not to take away from their historic fight or all their advocacy work since. While religion did play a factor in the courts' denial of their marriage license, it did not factor into the analysis of the ways that their marriage was historic.

The question of what power the U.S. Supreme Court's ruling had against them also remained. Different courts read it in different ways. As late as 2014, the decision was being cited as proof that bans on same-sex marriage were legal. However, other courts found that as the legal interpretations had changed, the decision was no longer precedent. All that was rendered moot in 2015, when, as part of the *Obergefell* decision, the U.S. Supreme Court directly overruled its previous *Baker* decision.

*See also:* *Baehr v. Miike*; Methodists; *Obergefell v. Hodges*; Religious Law and Practice in the United States Historically; 2000s, The

## Further Reading

*Baker v. Nelson*, 191 N.W.2d 185 (1971).
*Baker v. Nelson*, 409 U.S. 810 (1972).
Berger, Dan. (2010). *The Hidden 1970s: Histories of Radicalism*. New Brunswick, NJ: Rutgers University Press.

Frank, Nathaniel. (2017). *Awakening: How Gays and Lesbians Brought Marriage Equality to America*. Cambridge, MA: Belknap Press.

Hall, Simon. (2011). *American Patriotism, American Protest: Social Movements since the Sixties*. EBL-Schweitzer. Philadelphia: University of Pennsylvania Press.

Klarman, Michael J. (2013). *From the Closet to the Altar: Courts, Backlash, and the Struggle for Same-Sex Marriage*. Oxford, UK: Oxford University Press.

McConnell, Michael, Jack Baker, and Gail Karwoski. (2016). *The Wedding Heard "Round the World": America's First Gay Marriage*. Minneapolis: University of Minnesota Press.

Rupp, Leila J. (1999). *A Desired Past: A Short History of Same-Sex Love in America*. Chicago: University of Chicago Press.

## Baptist Church, The

With the Baptist Church, similar to other churches, it should be noted that there are many different branches of the church. This entry mostly discusses the Southern Baptist Convention (SBC) and its opposition to same-sex marriage. Other branches have different stances, but most Baptist churches in recent years have taken a stance in opposition to the practice.

The SBC is one of the more conservative churches. It also is one of the larger churches. It is clearly the largest Baptist group, and according to most estimates, it is the largest Protestant group. It is only smaller than the Catholic Church in terms of the number of members in the United States. The SBC formed before the Civil War when the Baptists split, largely over slavery, and the Southern Baptists have dominated the Baptists and stayed more southern ever since. (There have been moves to rename themselves something other than the Southern Baptist Convention, to use the initials for more than the name and to make "SBC" stand for other things than the Southern Baptist Convention.)

Southern Baptist views of marriage have generally been very traditional. Rather than supporting equality, the Baptists went with tradition. They followed the literal translation of the Bible and held that without man, women would not have existed. The man is also presented as the provider and protector. Baptists also believe that the man is parallel with the role that Jesus served founding the church, with the woman merely being the helper.

With that definition of marriage, it should be no surprise that same-sex marriage was and is not allowed in Southern Baptist theology. Marriage was defined by the church as the union of one man and one woman, with the woman submitting to the direction of her husband. Sex outside marriage is also banned, and so gay people have no way of having approved intimate relations. The church has also generally stood against same-sex relationships, as they are not presented as an acceptable lifestyle. However, marriage is not viewed as one of the sacraments (or, in Baptist terminology, *ordinances*). The difference is that Baptists believe that ordinances show obedience and sacraments give salvation. The two ordinances the Baptists generally believe in are baptism and Communion (also sometimes called the Lord's Supper).

Some have suggested that marriage is a civil rights issue and should be available to all. However, Southern Baptists disagreed. Not all clergy were fully certain of their views, and some have argued that this uncertainty is a good thing. Cadge et al. argued, "We are convinced of the analytic value of establishing a framework that provides space for uncertainty in our growing understanding of the relationship between religion and public opinion about homosexuality" (Cadge et al. 2012, 373). This uncertainty would allow change if clergy were able to publicly grapple with their views. It is unclear, though, whether clergy are going to be allowed this freedom of consideration.

The Southern Baptist views have also been slow to change in general. One historian noted that the SBC was one of last places in where segregation was publicly defended. Women are also not allowed to be pastors. Some churches that adopted female pastors have been removed from their local associations or state conventions. This level of traditionalism is part of why the church has been slow to allow people to be openly gay and lesbian, even though the issue has been discussed in general since the 1960s. Other areas were slow to change as well, as it took until the 1990s for the church to apologize for its defense of slavery, which the public had legally dropped over 100 years before.

It should be noted that some other Baptist churches have allowed same-sex marriages. In 2013, Allen wrote "an American Baptist church in Iowa City . . . announced that it [would] perform same-sex weddings" (Allen 2013). However, this Baptist church was affiliated with the Association of Welcoming and Affirming Baptists, a much smaller Baptist group that formed to welcome gay people as full members. Other smaller Baptist groups have also been more welcoming.

As far as what the future may hold, it is not clear. Membership in the SBC has been slowly dropping, in part due to its lack of change, with the membership down about 10 percent over the past decade. The real drop may have been more, as churches are not required to update their membership rolls, and if a congregation shifts to another fellowship, the SBC is not required to update its count. Thus, the real drop is probably more than that. It is unclear, though, whether the SBC would be motivated to update its ideas just to stay current with the times or to gain more members.

*See also:* Evangelicals; *Loving v. Virginia*; Methodists; Religion and Interracial Marriage; Religious Law and Practice in the United States Historically

## Further Reading

Allen, Bob. (2013). "Iowa Baptist Church Is Open to Gay Weddings." *The Christian Century*, January 17.

Brackney, William H. (2009). *The A to Z of the Baptists*. The A to Z Guide Series. Lanham, MD: Scarecrow Press.

Cadge, Wendy, Jennifer Girouard, Laura R. Olson, and Madison Lylerohr. (2012). "Uncertainty in Clergy's Perspectives on Homosexuality: A Research Note." *Review of Religious Research* 54 (3): 371.

Flynt, J. Wayne. (1998). *Alabama Baptists: Southern Baptists in the Heart of Dixie*. Religion and American Culture. Tuscaloosa: University of Alabama Press.

Kell, Carl L. (2014). *The Exiled Generations: Legacies of the Southern Baptist Convention Holy War*. Knoxville: University of Tennessee Press.

Kidd, Thomas S., and Barry Hankins. (2015). *Baptists in America: A History*. New York: Oxford University Press.

Morgan, David T. (1996). *The New Crusades, the New Holy Land: Conflict in the Southern Baptist Convention, 1969–1991*. Tuscaloosa: University of Alabama Press.

## *Burwell v. Hobby Lobby*

*Burwell v. Hobby Lobby* dealt with the question of when a governmental mandate could force certain types of companies to comply. Specifically, in this case, could the government force a corporation to provide contraceptive coverage when the owner of the corporation opposed that coverage on religious grounds? In 2014, the U.S. Supreme Court said no, as any restriction on religious liberty could only be justified by a compelling government objective and then only when the restriction was the only way to accomplish that objective (in this case, there were other ways to accomplish the same objective). This has implications for same-sex marriage, as many of the objections to same-sex marriage are based in religion. The question is, When can a government override a corporation's objections to same-sex marriage and force marriage equality?

Corporations with religiously oriented founders have always existed. However, health insurance benefits offered by those corporations have only recently reached the national spotlight. Part of that was due to the fact that insurance coverage itself was not that highly regulated before the 1990s. In turn, insurance is a relatively newer topic of interest. Most companies did not offer health insurance until the 1940s, when, during World War II, companies were allowed to add insurance without government oversight, while increases in pay were regulated. Due to the lack of regulation, there were no stipulations about what this insurance was required to cover. By the 1980s, insurance costs were skyrocketing, and companies were cutting costs, which meant lower coverage and higher premiums. As a response, people started noticing that a large percentage of Americans were without coverage and that their own coverage was inadequate.

Pressure mounted for a guarantee of insurance coverage and for that insurance to be adequate. Bill Clinton tried to mandate coverage in the 1990s, and Barack Obama took up the issue again in the 2008 presidential election. Obama urged Congress to pass mandatory health insurance requirements in the Affordable Care Act. Only then did attention shift to the specific provisions of an individual's insurance and what was required to be covered. Among other provisions was a requirement that contraceptives, including some IUDs and emergency contraceptives, be covered by private employers. Some employers, including Hobby Lobby, objected to these provisions, as they said they violated their faith. The founder of Hobby Lobby was an evangelical Christian and a member of the Seventh-day Adventist Church. Corporations had long been treated like persons in some parts of the law, but not all. For instance, corporations could not be found guilty of murder, and if a corporate executive committed a crime, the corporation was shielded from criminal liability. However, corporations could claim "religious freedom" when making decisions for their employees.

In 1993, Congress passed the Religious Freedom Restoration Act (RFRA), which required government regulations that burdened religion to use the least restrictive means. This law had been passed in response to a government case in which an individual using peyote had been penalized. Thus, a law passed to help an individual was now being used to protect a corporation. In the 2014 court case, Hobby Lobby also claimed that its religious freedom as an individual was threatened.

*Burwell v. Hobby Lobby* went all the way to the U.S. Supreme Court. The court found in favor of Hobby Lobby, but it did not focus that much on whether a corporation's religious liberty was threatened. Instead, it addressed whether the Affordable Care Act used the least restrictive means within its contraceptive provisions. As the U.S. government did allow some nonprofits to avoid the requirement through a work-around, it could have allowed Hobby Lobby to do this as well. The employees were still covered, but the insurance company simply paid for the coverage rather than charging the company. In an interesting twist, two of the four products objected to had been covered by the company's insurance before the Affordable Care Act. Either having something mandated made it more objectionable or else the corporation had failed to realize earlier that the coverage included the objectionable products.

Not all corporations were allowed this option, as only closely held companies were specifically treated in this fashion. Closely held corporations are companies with only a few majority stockholders. They are different from privately held companies, whose stock is not traded. While the definition seems to suggest that few companies would be affected by this, some analyses indicate that as many as 50 percent of corporations could be considered closely held, which means that a lot of companies may qualify for this treatment. After the *Hobby Lobby* decision, it was also unclear whose rights were being upheld. Was it just the owner, or were there other constituencies as well? Spencer Churchill wrote, "Although corporate standing served to vindicate the religious liberty of business owners in this case, the Court's reasoning justifies a right that is distinct from the rights of individual owners and that could potentially be grounded in the religious beliefs of a corporation's other constituencies" (2015, 437).

Anyone thinking that this case would end the issues of contraceptive coverage and religious liberty in insurance were sorely disappointed. By the end of the Obama administration, the Supreme Court was allowing employers to simply inform the government that they were not going to provide coverage, another step away from the original requirement. As of the time of this writing, the Biden administration was still finalizing its approach, although support for a contraceptive mandate was clear. There also remained questions of how broadly RFRA would be read after this or could be read. Marshall wrote, "Yet there are serious questions as to how, or whether, the Court's reading of RFRA in Hobby Lobby can be maintained in future cases. Indeed, there is significant question whether even a narrower interpretation of RFRA, such as the one offered by the dissenters in Hobby Lobby, which would only restore the pre-Smith case law, could realistically be maintained going forward" (2015, 74).

The case also had implication for same-sex marriage. If corporations could discriminate based on religion, as occurred here, could corporations discriminate against those who either were in same-sex marriages or wanted same-sex marriages to be performed? Can a corporation decide not to offer benefits to those in same-sex marriages while giving them to those in opposite-sex marriages? Or can a corporation offer wedding services to opposite-sex couples and deny them to same-sex couples? One deals with a multitude of companies while organizing and planning one's wedding. The questions remain once married, of course; for example, could a realtor refuse to serve a same-sex couple?

The overall underlying questions still remain as well. Is a corporation a person when considering religious freedom? Can a corporation avoid a law simply because the religious beliefs of its founder run counter to that law? And if the answer to both of these questions is yes (and the corporation in question is a closely held corporation and so exempt), where does that religious exemption end? The other underlying debate is to what extent the issue of religion can be used to thwart the legitimate goals of government. As noted, insurance coverage was not as large of a religious issue until it was mandated. Some corporations even covered the contraceptives and only objected after the mandate. One must wonder whether a company can object to a mandate when it was voluntarily doing (even if perhaps unknowingly) that same conduct before. One also wonders to what extent religion is the key issue here versus an overall objection to the larger government mandate.

**See also:** *Masterpiece Cakeshop v. Colorado Civil Rights Commission;* New Bills Opposing Same-Sex Marriage; *Obergefell v. Hodges;* 2000s, The

## Further Reading

Churchill, Spencer. (2015). "Whose Religion Matters in Corporate RFRA Claims after *Burwell v. Hobby Lobby Stores, Inc.,* 134 S. Ct. 2751 (2014)?" *Harvard Journal of Law & Public Policy* 38 (1): 437–450.

Epps, Garrett. (2014). *American Justice 2014: Nine Clashing Visions on the Supreme Court*. Philadelphia: University of Pennsylvania Press.

Gill, Emily R. (2019). *Free Exercise of Religion in the Liberal Polity: Conflicting Interpretations*. New York: Palgrave MacMillan.

Marshall, William P. (2015). "Bad Statutes Make Bad Law: Burwell v. Hobby Lobby." *Supreme Court Review* 2014 (1): 71.

Sands, Kathleen M. (2019). *America's Religious Wars: The Embattled Heart of Our Public Life*. New Haven, CT: Yale University Press.

Volokh, Eugene. (2014). *Sebelius v. Hobby Lobby: Corporate Rights and Religious Liberties*. Washington, DC: Cato Institute.

Von Hagel, Alisa, and Daniela Mansbach. (2016). *Reproductive Rights in the Age of Human Rights: Pro-Life Politics from Roe to Hobby Lobby*. New York: Palgrave Macmillan.

# Buttigieg, Pete

Pete Buttigieg, or "Mayor Pete," as he is better known, was the first major party presidential candidate who was both openly gay and Christian. The reason he is called "Mayor Pete" is because his last name is seen as difficult to pronounce. Gay rights activist Fred Karger ran for the Republican nomination for president in 2012, but he failed to finish above fourth in any primary and raised less than $100,000 for his campaign in outside funds. Buttigieg raised millions of dollars for his campaign. Karger was also not publicly identified as a Christian, unlike Mayor Pete. Mayor Pete finished fifth overall in the 2020 primaries, and he narrowly won Iowa, marking the first win for an openly gay presidential candidate.

Pete Buttigieg graduated from Harvard University in 2004 and then became a Rhodes Scholar. He joined the U.S. Navy Reserves and served from 2009 to 2017. While in the reserves, he deployed to Afghanistan. In many ways, Buttigieg reflects the larger picture of LGBTQ politics in that he won the mayoral race for South Bend in 2011 and then came out as gay. He was reelected as mayor in 2015, and the press coverage did not focus on his sexuality. During his time as mayor, he was viewed as a rising star in the Democratic Party.

Buttigieg identifies as an Episcopalian, though he was raised as a Catholic. He married his husband in 2018. As most, if not all, of his opponents for the Democratic nomination also supported same-sex marriage, it was not an issue at any of the public forums or debates. However, it was an issue on the campaign trail. At one appearance, someone heckled him from the audience, and rather than having the person removed, Buttigieg noted that he had fought in Afghanistan for the protestor's right to heckle. The treatment of hecklers was quite different from the stance of Donald Trump during his rallies.

Most of Buttigieg's opinions mirrored those of at least some of his rivals. However, he somewhat emphasized his youth and being part of the millennial generation, including his support for same-sex marriage.

In 2019, one study found that only 50 percent of those polled thought that the United States was ready for a gay or lesbian president (Morning Consult and Politico 2019). Other studies have found that most people say they are ready for one, which means that one of two things is going on, in addition to a possible polling error. First, the people being polled could be misreading their neighbors. Second, the people themselves could be thinking, "I'm supposed to be accepting of gays and lesbians, but I'm not. So I'll tell them that I'm ready but my neighbors are not." This is what is called *confirmation bias*.

There is reasonably good data that many Republicans are not ready to vote for a gay candidate. Some 40 percent in some polls have said that they would not vote for any gay candidate, which limited Mayor Pete's (or any other gay or lesbian candidate's) crossover appeal (Thomson-DeVeaux 2019). This poses a problem to any candidate, but particularly one for president, as the presidential vote in the Electoral College will probably come down to a few states where crossover votes are clearly needed. Losing out on any chance to get 50 percent of potential crossover candidates is a significant hardship. Of course, the polls may be wrong.

In the area of same-sex marriage, there was much hue and cry before the *Obergefell* decision and even some continuing opposition after it. This opposition and outcry came well after most of the United States had accepted (and elected) openly gay candidates. From this, one might expect there to be more opposition to a gay candidate who is married than one who is not, but the polls do not seem to bear this out. Of course, it would be the height of hypocrisy to say that, as most Americans seem to prefer a married president, even if the issue has not been extensively polled. For those polled to prefer a married straight president but a single gay or lesbian president would be over the top.

It should be noted that most presidents throughout history have been married, with only one being a bachelor (Buchanan) and another marrying during his first term (Cleveland). Widowers and those who were widowed while president have been more common. It should also be noted that only two people who have been divorced have been president (Trump and Reagan). Thus, throughout the history of the issue, marriage seems important, but it does not seem to have added an impediment to Buttigieg, despite opposition to same-sex marriage in general in recent years in varying amounts.

**See also:** Catholic Church, The; Episcopalians; *Obergefell v. Hodges*; 2004 Elections and Religion; 2000s, The

## Further Reading

Freedman, Estelle B. (2006). *Feminism, Sexuality, and Politics: Essays. Gender and American Culture*. Chapel Hill: University of North Carolina Press.

Haugen, David M., and Matthew J. Box. (2006). *Homosexuality*. Social Issues Firsthand. Farmington Hills, MI: Greenhaven Press,

Lampo, David. (2012). *A Fundamental Freedom: Why Republicans, Conservatives, and Libertarians Should Support Gay Rights*. Lanham, MD: Rowman & Littlefield Publishers.

Morning Consult and Politico. (2019). "National Tracking Poll 191058." Politico, October 25–28, 2019. https://www.politico.com/f/?id=0000016e-1976-d4da -a1ff-1bf676e00000.

Mucciaroni, Gary. (2008). *Same-Sex, Different Politics: Success and Failure in the Struggles over Gay Rights*. Chicago Studies in American Politics. Chicago: University of Chicago Press.

Stewart-Winter, Timothy. (2016). *Queer Clout: Chicago and the Rise of Gay Politics*. Politics and Culture in Modern America. Philadelphia: University of Pennsylvania Press.

Thomson-DeVeaux, Amelia. (2019). "Are Some Democratic Voters Reluctant to Support a Gay Candidate?" FiveThirtyEight, November 7, 2019. https:// fivethirtyeight.com/features/are-some-democratic-voters-reluctant-to-support -a-gay-candidate/.

# C

## Catholic Church, The

The Catholic Church has long condemned same-sex attraction, even though the emphasis was not that significant before the 4th century. It should also be noted that many of the early prohibitions mostly dealt with men having a same-sex attraction to young boys rather than just general prohibitions, and women were less regulated. The Catholic Church has largely continued this prohibition into the era of same-sex marriage.

Moving into the Middle Ages, penalties that had been mostly applied against clergy became generally applied. Also, the term *sodomy* was widely used to condemn all sexual intercourse that was not aimed at producing children, and many were turned over to the various inquisitions to be dealt with. Those who were gay or lesbian were often listed as being outside the protection of the church, and many national councils came to condemn same-sex attraction. However, some wanted to counsel those who confessed the crime, while others wanted them handed over to the state or excommunicated or sometimes burned at the stake.

After a time, the issue moved out of the public spotlight, until the time of Pope John Paul II, who condemned same-sex acts even while acknowledging "homosexual orientation" as not being a matter of choice. Those attitudes remained for most of the next 20 years, and both Pope John Paul II and Pope Benedict XVI spoke out against same-sex marriage.

Into the 21st century, it has been noted that the Catholic Church had a quite different conception of marriage and the purpose of marriage than the court system. One writer described the 2003 Massachusetts court decision and the Catholic Church's brief opposing it as follows: "Catholic teaching places the life of children in an exalted position in God's plan for man and woman. The Court, on the other hand, recognizes the importance children can play in a committed relationship, but places a much less substantial emphasis on procreation and child rearing as fundamental to marriage. And the Court obviously rejects sexual complementarity as at all essential to the marital relationship. The Court sees marriage as the union of two consenting adults of opposite or same gender, built upon mutual commitment and sharing" (Cunningham 2005, 22).

However, some change did start to occur with Pope Francis. The pope still opposed same-sex marriage but did not speak out as strongly against gay and lesbian people, and he also welcomed the children of same-sex couples into the church for baptism.

The Catholic Church is not united, though. A number of different groups have formed to minister to gay and lesbian Catholics. The earliest of these was Dignity USA, which was formed in the 1960s or the early years right after the start of the gay and lesbian rights movement following the Stonewall Riots of 1969. Another group that followed was Call to Action. These groups were met with varying responses from the U.S. Catholic leadership, with some priests and bishops working to excommunicate all those who associated with them.

As far as same-sex marriage, the Catholic Church initially opposed the efforts. In both Massachusetts and California, two of the larger and more urban states to consider same-sex marriage, the Catholic Church led the resistance to same-sex marriage. In California, the Catholic Church worked with the Mormons to oppose it and galvanize opposition. In recent years, the leadership in the United States has been more divided. In 2013, the bishop of Springfield, Illinois, called support for same-sex marriage "blasphemous," and in 2018, the archbishop of Chicago worked to stop a local priest from burning a gay pride flag. This shows that the issue is still open for discussion in the United States.

Pope Francis is also slowly moving on the issue. As noted before, he has allowed for the baptism of children of same-sex marriages when those marriages were performed civilly (not in the church). He has also called for respect for all people and stated that all people should be free from violence. This is a huge movement from the teachings of Pope John Paul II, just a few decades before. Pope Francis also said, "If a person is gay and he searches for the Lord and has good will, who am I to judge?" (Davis 2013). In general, Pope Francis has called for the church to have less condemnation of same-sex marriages and gays and lesbians in general. He even noted that there have been gay people throughout history. He seems to be, on this issue as on others, trying to not revise Catholic teachings too extensively while keeping it relevant for the 21st century.

*See also:* Baptist Church, The; Methodists; Presbyterians; Religious Law and Practice in the United States Historically; Sodom and Gomorrah

## Further Reading

Bordeyne, Philippe. (2006). "Homosexuality, Seen in Relation to Ecumenical Dialogue: What Really Matters to the Catholic Church." *New Blackfriars* 87 (1012): 561.

Cunningham, Maurice T. 2005. "Catholics and the ConCon: The Church's Response to the Massachusetts Gay Marriage Decision." *Journal of Church and State* 47 (1): 19.

Davis, Lizzy. (2013). "Pope Francis Signals Openness toward Gay Priests." *The Guardian*, July 29, 2013.

Gramick, Jeannine, and Pat Furey. (1988). *The Vatican and Homosexuality: Reactions to the "Letter to the Bishops of the Catholic Church on the Pastoral Care of Homosexual Persons."* New York: Crossroad.

Kirby, Brenda J., and Christina Michaelson. (2008). "Educating about Homosexuality: What Do American Catholics Think?" *Sex Education: Sexuality, Society and Learning* 8 (2): 225–235.

Lunch, John. (2005). "Institution and Imprimatur: Institutional Rhetoric and the Failure of the Catholic Church's Pastoral Letter on Homosexuality." *Rhetoric and Public Affairs* 8 (3): 383.

McNeill, John J. (1993). *The Church and the Homosexual.* 4th ed. Boston: Beacon Press.

Pizzuto, Vincent. 2008. "God Has Made It Plain to Them: An Indictment of Rome's Hermeneutic of Homophobia." *Biblical Theology Bulletin* 38 (4): 163–183.

Torevell, David. (2019). *"Angels in America*—A Theological Reading in Conjunction with Pope Francis' Apostolic Exhortation on the Call to Holiness in Today's World, *Gaudete et Exsultate* (Rejoice and Be Glad), and Key Catholic Writings on Homosexuality." *New Blackfriars* 100 (1088): 434–451.

# Chalcedon Movement

The Chalcedon Movement aims to make the state subservient to the church and is named after a 5th-century council, the Council of Chalcedon, which stated just that. As far as its connection to same-sex marriage, the movement is very much against same-sex attraction. As a matter of fact, it has called for the death penalty for same-sex relationships.

The Chalcedon Foundation was founded to advance these ideas, and it got its start from Rousas John (R. J.) Rushdoony, an author and minister. Rushdoony was originally in the Presbyterian Church of the United States of America, but he moved his affiliation to the Orthodox Presbyterian Church in 1957. The Orthodox Presbyterian Church opposed modernism, and Rushdoony had moved to oppose state power. He also argued that people were unable to think independent of God and that God had produced all knowledge. This was somewhat of a circular argument, as anything produced to dispute Rushdoony was held to be a sin and invalid, and so Rushdoony, in the eyes of his followers, must have been right.

In 1962, Rushdoony left his church and took up writing full time. In 1965, he started the Chalcedon Foundation. Among the main authors he worked with was Gary North. While this might seem to be a fringe movement, at its height, it had 12 full-time staff members and a sizable membership. The mailing list had tens of thousands of names, and Rushdoony claimed his movement had millions of followers. The books were also promoted by well-known figures such as Jerry Falwell and Pat Robertson. Sizable donors to the foundation included Nelson Hunt, an oil magnate, and Howard Ahmanson, a banker. The foundation's *Chalcedon Report* publication was renamed *Faith for All of Life* in 2005.

Among the ideas advanced by Rushdoony and his successors was a return to Old Testament biblical law. Among those laws that Rushdoony supported was the death penalty for lying and for same-sex attraction. It should be noted that the Bible allows for the death penalty by stoning for a wide variety of offenses. By some counts, there are over 30 crimes that allow this penalty, including working on the Sabbath. Today, that would ban work for three days, as some hold the Sabbath to be Friday (Judaism), some Saturday, and some Sunday. While Rushdoony did not call for all of these, it is difficult to see how the death penalty would be allowed for some capital crimes specified in the Old Testament but not for others. One writer noted that "Rushdoony did envision a society in which non-Christians who practiced their faith would be executed" (Worthen 2008, 401). Rushdoony called for both reconstructionism, where Christians have to rule the earth for 1,000 years to bring about the Second Coming, and dominionism, which holds that the common law of the Bible is the only law allowed.

While Rushdoony himself was not well known, the Moral Majority was linked to many of his views, and the Moral Majority played a large role in the rebirth of the conservative movement. Figures such as Jerry Falwell were vital in Ronald Reagan's election. Reagan, in turn, has been the key figure in the conservative movement of the last 40 years, with all presidential candidates either linked to him or active in his era.

The Chalcedon Foundation has published material attacking same-sex marriage. (Rushdoony himself died in 2001, and most of his published writing stopped in the early 1990s, before the same-sex marriage movement became active.) One review of a book entitled *What's Wrong with Same-Sex Marriage* praised it and noted, "This work should be placed into the hands of those swayed by secular arguments or those who do not understand their heterosexual marriage from the start by failing to consider a Biblical perspective" (Snapp 2004). The book argues that gay and lesbian people need to be converted, which would (presumably) end same-sex attraction and the need for same-sex marriage. Articles on the website also preach against same-sex marriage. Very few, though, come right out and call for anyone in a same-sex marriage to be stoned to death. The authors merely place their articles on the same site as a book calling for a return to the biblical law. One writer did note that "as adultery requires the death penalty under God's law, so too do other specific acts of fornication: rape, homosexuality, and incest" (Schwartz 2015).

There have been some people who have somewhat repudiated Rushdoony's ideas, but most seem to hope that the connection is not noticed. It is clear, though, that at least some of the people who support the Republican Party would do more than just end same-sex marriage if they came into power. To what extent these ideas would really be attempted is unclear, but the ideas are clearly still a part of the Republican Party's base.

*See also:* AIDS; Generational Differences; Religious Law and Practice in the United States Historically; Sodom and Gomorrah

## Further Reading

Blumenthal, Max. (2009). *Republican Gomorrah: Inside the Movement That Shattered the Party*. New York: Nation Books.

Ingersoll, Julie. (2015). *Building God's Kingdom: Inside the World of Christian Reconstruction*. New York: Oxford University Press.

McVicar, Michael. (2018). *Christian Reconstruction: R. J. Rushdoony and American Religious Conservatism*. Chapel Hill: University of North Carolina Press.

Rushdoony, Rousas J. (2002). *The Nature of the American System*. Vallecito, CA: Ross House Books.

Schwartz, Andrea. (2015). "Moving the Ancient Boundaries." Chalcedon, March 8, 2015. https://chalcedon.edu/magazine/moving-the-ancient-boundaries.

Snapp, Byron. (2004). "A Review of 'What's Wrong with Same-Sex Marriage?'" *Chalcedon*, September 1, 2014. https://chalcedon.edu/resources/articles/a-review-of-whats-wrong-with-same-sex-marriage.

Sutton, Matthew. (2014). *American Apocalypse*. Cambridge, MA: Harvard University Press.

Worthen, Molly. (2008). "The Chalcedon Problem: Rousas John Rushdoony and the Origins of Christian Reconstructionism." *Church History* 77 (2): 399–437.

# Church Schools

Many churches have long had their own religious schools. Most of the early church schools were Catholic or Jewish, with some being mostly at night or on Saturdays. With these schools, generally owned by the religious institution and sometimes on the religious institution's grounds, the question becomes how much power does a church have over the school? To look at the question another way is to ask when the decision of the religious entity can be scrutinized by the secular power.

A short look back on the history of church schools is helpful. Many early schools had a strong religious goal in general. Most early towns were Protestant, particularly in New England, where the educational movement was the strongest, and one of the goals of the schools was to teach reading (as one of the three R's). The goal in teaching reading was often largely for a fourth R—religion. If one was to read the Bible, as was supposedly the goal of every good Protestant, one needed to be able to read. This tied into the reading material in most homes, which was often only a Bible and an almanac. Bible verses were often used in schools as well.

Bible verses were mandated in the 19th century. The goal of these verses was both to create order and to spread religion. The religion was not being spread to the Protestant majority but to the Catholic and Jewish minorities. This often erupted into battles over which Bible to use, the Protestant King James Version or the Catholic Douay Version. The books in each varied, and those on both sides knew which one the schools should use—theirs. As most school boards were Protestant, most schools used the King James Bible, and many Catholics in turn formed their own schools. This helps to explain why most of the early religious schools were Catholic.

In the late 20th century, a variety of other private schools were founded. Some in the South were formed to maintain segregation, but a later wave was founded to keep away from the public school's teaching of evolution, which they opposed. Most of the schools in both groups were Protestant, in part because the Catholic Church did not oppose evolution and many areas already had a Catholic school. Also, many whites in communities moved wholesale from all-white public schools with a Protestant emphasis to all-white private schools, and so a Protestant emphasis would be expected.

These schools became involved in the same-sex marriage debate about the same time that the debate exploded across the country. Most of the schools were sponsored by religious entities that opposed same-sex marriage. When teachers and other figures spoke out in favor of same-sex marriage or married a same-sex partner, they were sometimes fired.

Some of the disputes rely on very narrow readings of the law. In one case dealing with a Protestant teacher who had been fired from a Catholic school because of her religion, the court allowed the firing because the school had noted, as an example in its handbook, that one was not allowed to remarry and switch religions (as this teacher had done) without the approval of the Catholic Church. Thus, since the teacher was warned, the firing was allowed. Marriage has often given workers more protection than free speech, in that religious institutions were generally allowed to fire workers for prohibited speech but were less likely to be allowed to fire workers for marrying in a way deemed improper.

The debate continues over what level of protection LGBTQ workers and those in same-sex marriages are given. Two cases in one city met with quite different results from the schools. One high school, after 22 months, decided to fire its teacher who was in a same-sex marriage because the local archdiocese said that if it did not, it would no longer be recognized as a Catholic school. Another high school decided to keep its teacher who is in a same-sex marriage and is appealing the archdiocese's ruling. Both schools are in Indianapolis, Indiana. The archdiocese's defense was that all the employees are ministers, and all ministers must follow the word of the church, including on same-sex marriage. In an interesting twist, the two teachers in the two cases are married to one another. The Vatican suspended the second school's expulsion from the diocese during the appeal.

Some schools seem to be more focused on their public image. For instance, the firing in Indianapolis only came after a Facebook post announcing the marriage. In another case, the San Francisco Archdiocese released a handbook ordering employees not to "visibly" oppose the church—in other words, no social media posts.

Religious schools have also been sued for announcing their views on same-sex marriage (and LGBTQ policy). One religious school in Maryland was removed from a school voucher program for having in its handbook an opposition to the idea that people can be transgender and opposition to the idea of same-sex marriage. The school contested the ban, proclaiming that the school had the right to announce its religious views.

*See also:* Catholic Church, The; Eastern Orthodox Church, The; History and Religion; Judaism; New Bills Opposing Same-Sex Marriage

## Further Reading

Long, Emma. (2018). "Yet Another Threat to Religious Freedom? Continuity and Change in the Church-State Debate." *Journal of Church & State* 60 (1): 1.

Mawdsley, Ralph D. (2011). "Employment, Sexual Orientation, and Religious Beliefs: Do Religious Educational Institutions Have a Protected Right to Discrimination in the Selection and Discharge of Employees?" *Brigham Young University Education and Law Journal* 2: 279.

"Minnesota Catholic School Teacher Fired over Marriage Equality Views." (2012). *Church & State* 65 (9): 20.

Oleske, J. M., Jr. (2015). "The Evolution of Accommodation: Comparing the Unequal Treatment of Religious Objections to Interracial and Same-Sex Marriages." *Harvard Civil Rights-Civil Liberties Law Review* 50 (1): 99–152.

Taylor, Derrick Bryson. (2019). "Jesuit School, Defying Archdiocese, Refuses to Fire Teacher in Gay Marriage." *New York Times*, June 21, 2019.

# Civil Rights Movement

The civil rights movement forced the United States to move forward in the area of civil rights for African Americans, particularly African American men. However, many other people labored in the shadows of that movement, and those people did not necessarily progress even at the slow speed of the civil rights march of those men. Those included African American women and the poor. Those groups were sometimes highlighted along the way, such as with Rosa Parks or the Poor People's Campaign that Dr. Martin Luther King Jr. was organizing in 1968 before he was assassinated. Other group also fought for the civil rights of those in the limelight but were ignored. Some of them have even been opposed when later asking for their own civil rights, including gay and lesbian Americans asking for same-sex marriage rights.

Even though it has not publicized (and was not publicized at the time), a sizable number of leading African American civil rights activists were gay. They included James Baldwin and Bayard Rustin. Rustin was closely involved in the civil rights movement. He was born in 1912 and so was older than some of the civil rights leaders of the 1960s. He had been active in the planned March on Washington movement of 1941 and also helped to organize the Freedom Rides. In the more well-known 1960s movement, Rustin helped to inform King about nonviolence.

In the 1950s, Rustin was arrested for having sex in public with another man, and this charge was frequently thrown against him by those opposed to civil rights. Some other civil rights leader either tried to change his sexual orientation or to marginalize him. After King's death, Rustin fought for gay rights somewhat in the 1980s.

Novelist James Baldwin was another gay civil rights activist. Baldwin did not label himself an activist, saying that demanding one's rights, to paraphrase him, was not being an activist. Baldwin was very active in the Student Nonviolent Coordinating Committee (SNCC) and the Congress for Racial Equality (CORE), but he was somewhat distant from King's efforts. This was due in part to King's view of same-sex attraction as a disease. Baldwin was also not fully embraced by the March on Washington in 1963 and was not allowed to speak at the end. Similar to Rustin, the overall civil rights movement was not that interested in working with Baldwin.

One might think that any marginalized minority would be interested in helping another, but that has not been the case in terms of gay and lesbian rights and the African American community. Part of this is due to most African American churches very much believing in the literal meaning of the Bible. This is because if the Bible was not literally true, it would have had very little value for African Americans. After all, if Moses had not really freed the Israelites, what hope was there for slavery ending? Another reason was because the civil rights movement was in many ways traditional; men led it, and many of the people in the forefront were middle class.

There were also strategic reasons in the 1960s for the civil rights movement to not support gay and lesbian causes. Many in the movement tried to stay away from anything that might weaken it, unless that decision brought a net gain of support. For instance, many in the movement tried to keep a safe distance from communism, even though the efforts did not stop those opposed to the movement from calling it communistic. However, both the marriage equality movement and the civil rights movement used much of the same language in calling for a return to the country's founding ideals rather than stepping away from them: "Rev. Dr. Martin Luther King, Jr., the movement's foremost leader, embodied the synergy of patriotism and protest that existed within the modern black freedom struggle. Throughout his public career King took great care to place demands for civil rights within a context that emphasized the gap between the nation's founding ideals and the reality of segregation and black disfranchisement" (Hall 2010, 538).

However, that does not explain why there was little support in the African American community in the 1990s and 2000s for same-sex marriage. The main reason appears to be that many valued religion over marriage equality and stuck to their guns. Even today, support for same-sex marriage in the African American community is relatively low, especially compared to other groups who share the same overall social views. When Massachusetts adopted same-sex marriage, some African American pastors denounced the move. "'African-Americans have to be who we are,' said Bishop Paul Morton Sr. of the Greater St. Stephen Full Gospel Baptist Church in New Orleans. 'This is the way we're going to heaven. They [gays and lesbians] don't have to go to heaven that way'" (Russell 2008, 101).

Thus, even though gay and lesbian people of all colors fought for the rights of African Americans, their sacrifices were not acknowledged at the time. Also, those sacrifices did not change attitudes in the African American community toward gay and lesbian people and same-sex marriage.

*See also:* Baptist Church, The; *Loving v. Virginia*; Religion and Interracial Marriage; Religious Law and Practice in the United States Historically

## Further Reading

Allitt, Patrick. (2003). *Religion in America since 1945: A History*. Columbia Histories of Modern American Life. New York: Columbia University Press.

Carnes, Mark C. (2002). *Invisible Giants: Fifty Americans Who Shaped the Nation but Missed the History Books*. New York: Oxford University Press.

Hall, Simon. (2010). "The American Gay Rights Movement and Patriotic Protest." *Journal of the History of Sexuality* 19 (3): 536.

Leeming, David Adams. (1994). *James Baldwin: A Biography*. New York: Knopf.

Mumford, Kevin J. (2016). *Not Straight, Not White: Black Gay Men from the March on Washington to the AIDS Crisis*. The John Hope Franklin Series in African American History and Culture. Chapel Hill: University of North Carolina Press.

Podair, Jerald E. (2009). *Bayard Rustin: American Dreamer*. The African American History Series. Lanham, MD: Rowman & Littlefield Pub.

Russell, Thaddeus. (2008). "The Color of Discipline: Civil Rights and Black Sexuality." *American Quarterly* 60 (1): 101–128.

# Civil vs. Religious Marriage

One major issue in the whole same-sex marriage debate is how much influence religion should have. As part of this, there is the issue of how religious a marriage should be. If a marriage was guaranteed to have religious elements, then religion would, in turn, be guaranteed a say in the formation and breakup of a marriage. In a marriage without guaranteed religious elements, religion would not be guaranteed a say.

This entry does not argue that marriage historically, both in the United States and elsewhere, has not had religious elements. In most religions, marriage is an important ceremony. It is one of the two sacraments recognized by nearly every Protestant church (along with baptism) and one of the seven sacraments recognized by Catholics, Hussites, Old Catholics (that is the name of the church), and the Eastern Orthodox Church.

Marriage is also a unique rite in that it is, in many places, one of the few available outside the church. In comparison, no magistrate will perform a baptism or a confirmation (although justices sometimes encounter a confession of sorts during a plea bargain). However, the justice of the peace does not give a religious deity's order of penance but the state's.

In the United States, marriage has always been the concern of the state, even when there was only one church generally allowed. This does not mean that marriages—or divorces, to look at the other end—were easily granted. However, the state was always in control of it, along with the parents. Parents, particularly the father, were allowed to control who came to see their daughters. The parents also controlled whether their daughter had a dowry or their son brought property into a marriage, both of which were expected in the upper class. The lower class saw less of this, as they had little property.

Another way to look at the issue is to determine who issues marriage licenses. In the United States, even while still a colonial possession of the British Crown, some places started issuing marriage licenses. In 1639, less than 20 years after the Pilgrims, marriage licenses were required in the colony of Massachusetts. In other places, it was later, but in the 17th century in general, they were issued in several places. Some states and colonies did require a marriage to be performed by a minister of the approved church, but this was only when the colony had a state religion. For instance, in Virginia, before 1781 (for the state since 1776 and the colony before that), a minister of the Church of England had to perform the marriage. However, there was an exception in Virginia (to stay with the same colony). One could marry if one provided a bond that assured the public that neither party was already married and that both were of age. Part of the reason for this exception was that there were not enough ministers in some places.

One can also look at who grants a divorce. While different states have different divorce requirements (Las Vegas was for a time the capital of quick marriage and quick divorces, as well as the events that caused the divorce), divorce has always been regulated by the state.

Many places also had common-law marriage. This is where two people live together for a certain amount of time and present themselves as being married but do not have a formal marriage certificate. About 10 states still have some variant of common-law marriage, and several others allow common-law marriages that were entered into before a certain date. Many people assume common-law marriage is still around today, even though it generally is not.

Common-law marriages used to be more common, as nearly three-fourths of the U.S. states allowed it at one time or another. If one did not even have to ask the state's permission, never mind the church's or synagogue's, to get married, this shows that religion did not play a deciding role. Common-law marriages also accounted for the fact that one was often far distant from a church or synagogue, never mind being close to a church or synagogue that lined up with one's own faith.

In relation to same-sex marriage, this shows that although many people's marriages take (and took) place in a church, synagogue, mosque, or temple, it is (and was) not required. It has also not generally been required in U.S. history. Thus, the argument that marriage is a religious institution and so should be subject to religious laws is wrong. Of course, even if it was, the question would be whose religion to use, and since some religions now allow same-sex marriage, there would be no guarantee of same-sex marriage being banned. Finally, while one might think that making marriage a religious decision would move the same-sex marriage debate out of the public sphere and decrease content, it would actually increase it, as it would bring to the forefront the debate of what makes a religion and whose religion should hold sway (if one religion got to pick for all). If one just had to be religious to get married in a house of worship, that would remove the second question, but, in turn, it would intensify the first.

***See also:*** Catholic Church, The; Defense of Marriage Act, The; Pastors vs. Their Churches; Religious Law and Practice in the United States Historically; Same-Sex Marriage Worldwide

## Further Reading

Babst, Gordon A., Emily R. Gill, and Jason Pierceson, eds. (2009). *Moral Argument, Religion, and Same-Sex Marriage: Advancing the Public Good*. Lanham, MD: Lexington Books.

Dolan, Frances E. (2008). *Marriage and Violence: The Early Modern Legacy*. Philadelphia: University of Pennsylvania Press.

Gill, Emily R. (2012). *An Argument for Same-Sex Marriage: Religious Freedom, Sexual Freedom, and Public Expressions of Civic Equality*. Religion and Politics Series. Washington, DC: Georgetown University Press.

Nock, Steven L., Laura Ann Sanchez, and James D. Wright. (2008). *Covenant Marriage: The Movement to Reclaim Tradition in America*. New Brunswick, NJ: Rutgers University Press.

Thornton, Arland, William G. Axinn, and Yu Xie. (2007). *Marriage and Cohabitation*. Population and Development. Chicago: University of Chicago Press.

# D

## Davis, Kim, and Other Clerks

Clerks have an important role to play in many courts. While the rule of law is often focused on judges and the Supreme Court, the day-to-day operations mostly occur at the local level. When clerks wish to imprint their own ideas on a local issue, they very often can. This is shown in part by the practice of electing clerks, rather than having them appointed, which is different from many other agencies. The person who runs the DMV is usually not elected, to give a comparison.

Kim Davis, a clerk in Rowan County, Kentucky, shot to international attention in 2015 when she refused to issue marriage licenses after the U.S. Supreme Court's ruling in *Obergefell*. Davis was elected clerk in 2014 but took office in 2015. She had been a long-term employee in the clerk's office. The reason that she gave for refusing to issue same-sex certificates was that she was opposed on religious grounds and the marriage certificate had her name on it. She then refused to issue any marriage certificates when she was told that she had to issue them for same-sex couples. Davis also argued that the governor was trying to violate her religious freedom by forcing her to issue those certificates. The issue finally ended with Davis being put in jail for contempt of court, and most of Davis's deputy clerks agreed to issue the certificates. After her release, she altered the marriage certificates to remove her name entirely. In 2019, she was voted out of office.

Davis was not the only clerk who was opposed to issuing the certificates. Two other clerks in Kentucky also refused, but they did not court publicity and refused to talk to a rally where Davis was also making an appearance. In other clerks' offices, "mysterious" delays in generating new forms stopped same-sex marriages, and some clerks resigned. The Alabama Supreme Court allowed 10 clerks to not issue marriage licenses, but Alabama has long allowed judges to refuse to marry anyone they did not want to.

Clerks in general are in a fairly unique position. Unlike judges, who are only needed when a ruling is performed, clerks (and their employees) interact with the public on a regular basis. Clerks are also generally elected and so must please the public, and they generally cannot be removed. While Davis could be put in jail for contempt of court, it was noted that it would be difficult to remove her. Once elected, she was in her term for the full four years. Some states may have ways to remove clerks, but Kentucky does not.

Clerks are unlikely to be checked by a state's attorney general in the area of same-sex marriage. Most states that have clerks who oppose same-sex marriage are states that oppose it as a whole (or mostly), like Alabama. In such a state, a popularly elected attorney general is not going to try to shut down a clerk like Kim Davis. The same is true of the governor, as shown by the governor of Kentucky in 2015, who moved to allow clerks to remove their name from marriage certificates. Thus, politics would probably limit any check on other clerks who wanted to follow Davis's example. However, Davis did lose her reelection bid in 2018.

Some other clerks have publicly opposed same-sex marriage and still kept their positions. In New York (a state seen as more liberal than Kentucky), a clerk denied a marriage license to a same-sex couple. The state enforced a $20,000 fine against the town, and the clerk issued an apology. As of 2021, the clerk is still serving.

Litigants are also going to have a difficult time contesting people like Kim Davis. The reason for this is that in many areas, those favoring same-sex marriage may not want to be in the public eye. Davis was somewhat unique in being in a conservative area where people were willing to be seen as challenging her. Such was obviously not the case elsewhere, as Davis was the only one sued.

Clerks also possess a power that limits challenges. A clerk's office can always just delay, and it is difficult to force action. This can be seen by those clerks who on this issue claimed to not have the forms revised yet. While that may have been the case, it might also have been a delaying tactic. Many people assume that if one drags their heels long enough, the issue will go away, particularly if there are other options for solving the issue. A clerk's office may assume that if one county ignores the issue, the same-sex couple will just go to a different county. That is sometimes echoed in public sentiment, which holds that the area is not opposed to same-sex marriage but just wishes the people would get married somewhere else.

Thus, clerks still have a large amount of power to slow marriage licenses, even though few will go as far as Davis. Of course, sources greatly vary, with biographies of Davis that favor her, such as the one produced by the Liberty Counsel cited in the further reading section, and portray her as a religious martyr, while the other side portrays her as bigoted. That fact, though, does not reduce the chilling effect that clerks can have, sometimes without easy recourse, on same-sex marriage.

*See also:* New Bills Opposing Same-Sex Marriage; *Obergefell v. Hodges*; Pentecostals; Religious Freedom Restoration Act; Religious Law and Practice in the United States Historically

## Further Reading

"Clerk Contest." (2018). *Christian Century* 1: 8.

Davis, Kimberly Jean. (2018). *Under God's Authority*. Orlando, FL: New Revolution Publishing.

"NY Clerk Re-Elected." (2011). National Catholic Reporter, November 25, 2011.

Silberman, Eve. (2007). "Agent of Change." *Public Management* 10: 28.

Williams, H. Howell. (2018). "From Family Values to Religious Freedom: Conservative Discourse and the Politics of Gay Rights." *New Political Science* 40 (2): 246–263.

# Defense of Marriage Act, The

The Defense of Marriage Act (better known as DOMA) did two things. First, no state was required to recognize any same-sex marriage from another state. Second, on the federal level, it held that in all laws, marriage only meant a marriage between a man and a woman. This was aimed at preventing the spread of same-sex marriage from one state to another.

DOMA was prompted in large part by a court decision in Hawaii. In 1993, the Hawaii Supreme Court ruled that the state constitution does not allow the denial of a marriage certificate to same-sex couples. This moved the issue to the forefront of LGBTQ rights advocacy. Although this was a state court decision based on state law, the nation became interested, as, in most cases in modern times, states respect each other's marriages and divorces. People in small-town Nebraska were suddenly interested in who could marry in faraway Hawaii. Religion played a role in that many people felt that their religion did not allow same-sex marriage. Congress considered a number of measures to deal with the controversy surrounding the Hawaii Supreme Court decision. Some argued for a federal constitutional amendment banning same-sex marriage, even though marriage has rarely been a federal law issue. However, a federal amendment was not introduced at the time.

In 1996, Congress did introduce DOMA, which passed with high support from both parties; every Republican but one favored it as well as two-thirds of all Democrats. Bill Clinton had pushed for issues favored by LGBTQ groups but still signed it. He argued that he was preventing a federal amendment on the issue; in reality, 1996 being a presidential election year probably played a larger role. Most religions at the time did not allow for same-sex marriage. For all practical purposes, Clinton's signature was academic, as both houses of Congress had passed the bill by solidly veto-proof majorities. Bill Clinton was roundly criticized for his decision to sign DOMA, but other politicians got a pass on their changes of thought, which mirrored most Americans. There was also a debate about how local law should influence the issue. Author Courtney Joslin argued that the status had long been federal: "There is a rich and wide web of federal laws that deeply impact and regulate families" (Joslin 2015, 788).

By 2000, both political parties were expected to take a stand on DOMA. However, while favored, Democrats did not mention the act. Several religious institutions had also started to allow same-sex marriage. One of the first religions to do this was the Unitarian Universalist Church. Same-sex marriages and other ceremonies occurred in TV shows, keeping the controversy in the eyes of the public.

In 2004, DOMA and opposition to same-sex marriage were major issues not only for individual states but also for Republican politicians. While John Kerry, the Democratic nominee for president, tried to keep away from the issue, the Republican party turned it into a major campaign issue. George Bush called for a constitutional amendment banning same-sex marriage, and some analysts think that Kerry's inability to stay away from the issue cost him the presidency. Bush became the only Republican in 28 years to win the popular vote in addition to winning the electoral vote. This showed the level of public thinking, particularly of those in the middle of the issue, in 2004.

At the same time, the nation was also slowly changing. The DOMA debate caused many LGBTQ advocates to become more active and visible. Lawsuits were filed against bans on same-sex marriage, even while measures opposed to same-sex marriage were winning and efforts challenging those bans snaked through the courts. Many states compromised with "marriage-light" measures, including domestic partnerships and civil unions; in some cases, they granted all the rights of marriage except the name. The name was important, though, not only for equality but also for the federal benefits and the ability to have the marriage recognized in other states. In 2000, in response to a lawsuit, Vermont became the first state to have same-sex civil unions, which was pushed through in response to a state supreme court decision. In 2003, Massachusetts became the first state to have same-sex marriage, once again in response to a state court ruling. Churches now had to decide whether to preside over and allow same-sex marriages and other ceremonies.

States were being pushed by their courts to have marriage equality, and by 2008, most states had decided. Two states had legalized it, and another 45 had banned it, either by a state constitutional amendment or statute. Most of the early states allowing same-sex marriage did so in response to state courts determining that their constitutions required marriage equality. Most of those states had voters somewhat in the middle; they did not reverse the court, but they obviously were not ready to equalize marriage without the court. The first states where voters approved of same-sex marriage, as shown by a statewide referendum, were Maine, Maryland, and Washington in 2012. By 2012, between the courts, the legislatures, and voters, nine states had adopted marriage equality.

The federal courts were also getting into the picture, as district courts and courts of appeals were dealing with objections to DOMA. President Obama also chose not to defend DOMA. "While it is rare for the executive branch not to defend a statute, the decision not to defend DOMA is consistent with executive branch determinations of the past and is wholly dictated by litigation posture and procedure (even if it may yield political dividends as a result of the timing). The resultant legal stance is practically and legally correct" (Robinson 2011, 702).

In 2013, the Supreme Court struck down DOMA as related to federal law, but this did not reach the issue of state law. That was finally resolved in 2015 in *Obergefell v. Hodges*, which declared same-sex marriage legal in all states and fully struck down DOMA. To show how public opinion was shifting, by 2015, 36 states had enacted marriage equality through the state legislatures, state courts, or federal courts. That was a sharp spike from 2 in 2008.

Religious perspectives also shifted. More churches announced support, and some churches sued (before *Obergefell*) to be allowed to marry people when state law prevented it.

**See also:** Baehr v. Miike; Masterpiece Cakeshop v. Colorado Civil Rights Commission; Obergefell v. Hodges; 2004 Elections and Religion; 2000s, The

## Further Reading

Ball, Carlos A. (2010). *From the Closet to the Courtroom: Five LGBT Rights Lawsuits That Have Changed Our Nation*. Boston: Beacon.

Becker, Jo. (2014). *Forcing the Spring: Inside the Fight for Marriage Equality*. New York: Penguin Press.

Chabora, Paige E. (1997). "Congress' Power under the Full Faith and Credit Clause and the Defense of Marriage Act of 1996." *Nebraska Law Review* 76 (3): 604.

Joslin, Courtney G. (2015). "Federalism and Family Status." *Indiana Law Journal* 90 (2): 787–828.

Robinson, Dustin F. (2011). "A Defense of Non-Defense of the Defense of Marriage Act." *Georgetown Journal of Gender & the Law* 12 (3): 701–710.

Strasser, Mark Philip, and NetLibrary, Inc. (1999). *The Challenge of Same-Sex Marriage: Federalist Principles and Constitutional Protections*. Westport, CT: Praeger. Ebook Central (Collection). Web.

Zott, Lynn M. (2012). *Church and State*. Detroit, MI: Greenhaven.

## *Dumont v. Gordon*

The *Dumont* case springs from a relatively recent Michigan law that held that religious groups could discriminate against same-sex couples in placing children. The ACLU sued Michigan over the law. The law was put into place in response to the *Obergefell* case working its way through the courts, which legalized same-sex marriage nationwide. In an interesting twist, the state waited until the *Obergefell* case to act, rather than looking at it before. The law also does not differentiate between unmarried same-sex couples and people in same-sex marriages, suggesting that the state did not value their marriages.

In 2018, the ACLU won a motion hearing, which suggested that the trial, if it came to that, would go in the favor of the ACLU and marriage equality. Based on that, Michigan decided to settle. "The state of Michigan announced on March 22, 2019, that it will require all taxpayer funded, state-contracted child welfare agencies to accept all qualified families, including same-sex couples" (ACLU 2019). One might wonder why Michigan settled when its law favored a different policy only a few years before. The reason was that the judge had basically indicated that the ACLU would win, and so the state saw little reason to keep fighting when a negotiated settlement would bring the same result quicker and more affordably. One might call this the practice of knowing how and when to lose gracefully.

Michigan was the first state to settle in this matter. Some states did allow same-sex couples to adopt, but they had not had recent bans. For instance, California has had adoption by same-sex couples since 2003 or, to put it another way, five years before it allowed same-sex marriages. Thus, Michigan was somewhat unique.

Other states had acted to allow agencies to discriminate based on their religious convictions. States had turned to these religious agencies to save money and also because this widened their base of potential adoptees, as some people trust a charity more than the state. Organizations also sometimes did a better job of advertising and had access to a more attentive population. States have, in turn, been reluctant to limit these churches, as the most active churches represent a large part of the voting population. Churchgoers are also more likely to vote, increasing their power.

In some states, same-sex marriage had only narrow support, meaning that groups were willing to allow same-sex marriage, but not too much of it. In turn, this meant that anyone opposed to it was looking for a way to discriminate. This included a ban on same-sex couples adopting under the guise of religious freedom. States such as Oklahoma and Kansas have worked to pass laws that allow agencies to not place children with same-sex couples if they have religious objections to it. The objections have to be "deeply held" in most bills, but that is, of course, a very amorphous term, as is the term religion, as past cases dealing with the First Amendment have shown.

In the past, other states restricted the ability of same-sex couples to adopt, putting their thumb on the scale. These included Arkansas, which did not allow unmarried couples to adopt. A single gay person could adopt but not couples. Other states, including Nebraska, had policies that favored married couples, but only same-sex unmarried couples had been affected.

One might expect conservatives, who oppose state involvement and welfare, to be more favorable toward same-sex adoption because it moves the children off state support. However, that has not been the case in general. (The following studies were not specific to Michigan.) One study found "neoliberal views—specifically, beliefs that the government is doing too much to solve the country's problems and unemployment subsidies should not be given to able-bodied persons . . . are associated with more negative views toward same-sex adoption among the general public, as well as political conservatives, Catholics, and liberal Protestants" (Perry and Whitehead 2015, 1739).

It should be noted that there has not been that much research into the children of same-sex couples who were adopted. Obviously, with same-sex marriage being a relatively new concept, less research has been done in that area. However, the research that has been done shows little difference between the children of same-sex couples and those of opposite-sex couples when dealing with adopted children. "No significant differences were found among child, parent, couple, or family adjustment as a function of parental sexual orientation when children were school-age, and effect sizes comparing family groups were smaller than those comparing change over time for the entire sample" (Farr 2017, 261).

Thus, the settlement in the *Dumont* case resolves the issue, for the time being at least, in Michigan, but it remains contested in other areas. Most states are not like Michigan and settle gracefully.

***See also:*** Adoption; Davis, Kim, and Other Clerks; *Obergefell v. Hodges*; Religious Freedom Restoration Act; Religious Law and Practice in the United States Historically

## Further Reading

ACLU. (2019). "*Dumont v. Gordon*." ACLU, March 22, 2019. https://www.aclu .org/cases/dumont-v-gordon.

Brodzinsky, David, and Adam Pertman. (2012). *Adoption by Lesbians and Gay Men: A New Dimension in Family Diversity*. New York: Oxford University Press.

Child Welfare Information Gateway. (2016). *Working with Lesbian, Gay, Bisexual, Transgender, and Questioning (LGBTQ) Families in Foster Care and Adoption*. Bulletin for Professionals. Washington, DC: U.S. Department of Health and Human Services, Children's Bureau.

Conn, Peter J. (2013). *Adoption: A Brief Social and Cultural History*. Palgrave Pivot. New York: Palgrave Macmillan.

Farr, Rachel H. (2017). "Does Parental Sexual Orientation Matter? A Longitudinal Follow-Up of Adoptive Families with School-Age Children." *Developmental Psychology* 53 (2): 252–264.

Masters, Lindsay. (2017). "Same-Sex Adoption in the Wake of Obergefell: How Recent Michigan Legislation Runs Counter to the First Amendment Rights of Prospective Adoptive Parents." *University of Detroit Mercy Law Review* 1: 99.

McQueen, Allison L. (2017). "Michigan's Religious Exemption for Faith-Based Adoption Agencies: State-Sanctioned Discrimination or Guardian of Religious Liberty?" *Notre Dame Law Review* 2: 895.

Perry, Samuel L., and Andrew L. Whitehead. (2015). "Same-Sex Adoption as a Welfare Alternative? Conservatism, Neoliberal Values, and Support for Adoption by Same-Sex Couples." *Journal of Homosexuality* 62 (12): 1722–1745.

# E

## Eastern Orthodox Church, The

By the Eastern Orthodox Church, this entry is referring to the church that started in the 1st century and is currently headquartered, somewhat, in Turkey. In many ways, this church achieved most of its current structure in the 11th century, when it fully split from the Catholic Church (or the Catholic Church split from it, depending on which side of the controversy you read). Similar to the Catholic Church, the Eastern Orthodox Church traces its beginning back to the original apostles. There are other branches of Christianity that label themselves "Orthodox," but those are not being discussed here, except as noted.

The Eastern Orthodox Church generally considers same-sex attraction to be a sin and so does not allow same-sex marriage. The church has also strongly spoken out against same-sex marriage. In most church documents, same-sex attraction is put on the same level as adultery and fornication, and in some churches, it is viewed at the same level as sexual assault. Unlike some churches, the Eastern Orthodox Church does not have a formal head, but the leading patriarch is in Turkey, being the successor to the patriarch at what was once Constantinople (now Istanbul). However, regardless of structure, all the leading figures of the traditional mainline Eastern Orthodox Church condemn same-sex attraction. Similar to this, the Eastern Orthodox Church is also not welcoming of same-sex marriage. Unlike some churches, there is no evidence of many Eastern Orthodox Churches who are welcoming to gay people, even while not allowing them to be full members. This is the pattern that most Eastern Orthodox Churches in the United States fall into.

There is also the question of what churches outside of the United States do. Many countries that are mostly Eastern Orthodox and that allow the church to have power also have some level of a ban on same-sex marriage and some repression of gay people. One of those countries is Greece, where same-sex marriage is not allowed, even though there are antidiscrimination provisions. Greece also has little religious influence in the public sphere. Other countries with more repression include the Ukraine, where social attitudes oppose gay people. There is public opposition (even though that opposition is decreasing) to same-sex marriage; it is not allowed, and there do not appear to be any immediate plans to allow it.

Factors outside religion also play a role. The European Union has mandated antidiscrimination policies. Ukraine wants to join the European Union and so has been moving toward improving the treatment of people who are gay or lesbian. There are also nations that have a high number of people who believe in Eastern Orthodox Christianity, but the nation itself is not interested in the people's direct opinion. Those would include Russia, which is, by most independent accounts, a dictatorship. The Eastern Orthodox Church is a majority of the people in only about a dozen countries, and there is a significant number, but not a majority, in more.

It should be noted that not all people who consider themselves to be Orthodox Christians condemn same-sex attraction. Some Orthodox churches outside of the central structure are more welcoming, and there is an Orthodox-Catholic Church of America that welcomes people who are gay or lesbian. However, those churches though are generally smaller. The Orthodox-Catholic Church of America has about 300 churches, while the Orthodox Church has about 1,400, although counts vary.

Thus, the Eastern Orthodox Church as a whole generally does not support gay people, and so it should come as no surprise that same-sex marriages are opposed as well. There are some churches with some of the same ideas that support equality and same-sex marriage, but they are smaller. Unlike other denominations, this policy is set at the national level rather than being left to each individual church or parish to decide.

*See also:* Baptist Church, The; Catholic Church, The; Mormons; Religious Law and Practice in the United States Historically

## Further Reading

Casiday, Augustine. (2012). *The Orthodox Christian World.* Routledge Worlds. Abington, UK: Routledge.

Demacopoulos, George E., and Aristotle Papanikolaou. (2017). *Christianity, Democracy, and the Shadow of Constantine.* Orthodox Christianity and Contemporary Thought. New York: Fordham University Press.

Manoussakis, John Panteleimon. (2016). "Marriage and Sexuality in the Light of the Eschaton: A Dialogue between Orthodox and Reformed Theology." *Religions* 7 (7): 89.

McGrath, Alister E. (2012). *Christian History: An Introduction.* New York: Wiley.

"Statement from the Assembly of Canonical Bishops of North and Central America on Same-Sex Unions." (2013). *Greek Orthodox Theological Review* 58 (1–4): 354–355.

# Episcopalians

The Episcopal Church originated in many ways from one event and one man. The man was Henry VIII, who wanted a divorce so that he might remarry and have a son for an heir, and so he separated from the Catholic Church and created the Church of England. The Episcopal Church split from the Church of England due to the American Revolution. The Church of England swore allegiance to the king of England, and so the U.S. Episcopal Church split off. The church in the United States has become more generally liberal than its Church of England founder and even more liberal than its other fellow churches in the Anglican Communion, to which it belongs. This entry discusses the Episcopal Church headquartered in New York City, not the smaller branches headquartered elsewhere. The New York City church has about 1.5 million active members.

The 20th century saw a general liberalization of Episcopal doctrine. Many Episcopal priests marched for civil rights in the 1950s and 1960s, with some becoming martyrs. The church battled over ordaining women and LGBTQ priests, but it ordained both by the end of the 1970s. Over the next 40 years, the questions of LGBTQ leadership and same-sex marriage continued. Despite being liberal, movement was slow on LGBTQ leadership. The first LGBTQ priest was ordained in 1977, but it took until 2003 for the first LGBTQ bishop to be put into place—and that was over the objections of the worldwide Anglican Communion. That bishop, Gene Robinson, was subjected to many death threats. It took until 2006 for the U.S. Episcopal Church to have its first woman leader.

In general, Episcopalian views on same-sex attraction changed slowly, as noted, as did their views on same-sex marriage when that came to the forefront. In 1976, the Episcopal Church held that those who were gay were still "children of God," and it called for equal rights and treatment for gay people. It also treated them as members of the church, unlike some denominations. Gay and lesbian individuals also became priests in this period, as noted. However, the Episcopal Church in the 1990s still held that sex was only supposed to take place in marriage, thus dooming any Episcopalian, priest or otherwise, to a loveless life, as there was no same-sex marriage at the time. (The regulation was not aimed against gay and lesbian people as much as against unmarried people, but, of course, there was no option for gay people to marry.)

As the same-sex marriage debate heated up, the U.S. Episcopal Church moved somewhat slowly, especially considering its earlier stance on gay people. It was not until nearly the end of the first decade of the 2000s that the church moved to develop materials for ceremonies celebrating same-sex couples (but not materials for same-sex weddings yet) and that the church told the local priests to provide counseling for same-sex couples. In 2015, the church completed the circuit and changed the definition of *marriage* to allow same-sex couples to marry in the Episcopal Church. Similar to other areas of this issue, the wider Anglican Church did not like the ruling and protested it; it even temporarily suspended some of the U.S. leaders. In the United States, some churches left the Episcopal Church and affiliated themselves with other branches.

The Episcopal Church is one of the more welcoming churches. It has both gay and lesbian priests and allows for same-sex marriage. It also allows for counseling of same-sex couples. In terms of adoptions, it was very welcoming and supported those who adopted and were in same-sex marriages. The Episcopal Church has also been more willing than some to address past errors. It apologized for its part in slavery in 2006 and for its lack of action in opposing racism in the American South. It should be noted that in the 1960s, the Episcopalians were more active than some in the civil rights movement. Thus, the move to change their stances and be open about it is not limited to same-sex relationships.

Episcopalians were also sometimes more willing to separate policy from morality than other groups. In a study of one New York Episcopal Church, the authors noted that the issue was thought of as based in civil rights: "Thus, the contested comparisons and framings of LGBTQ rights as similar to other civil rights struggles appear to have a strategic value insofar that they provide a framework for thinking around difference in terms that can be detached from issues of private sexual-religious morality" (Andersson et al. 2013, 257). The Episcopalians, willing to think of things in a different way, opened up new ways to reconcile their religion and same-sex marriage and also came to rethink religion.

*See also:* Adoption; Baptist Church, The; Catholic Church, The; Religious Law and Practice in the United States Historically

## Further Reading

Andersson, Johan, Robert M. Vanderbeck, Joanna Sadgrove, Gill Valentine, and Kevin Ward. (2013). "Same-Sex Marriage, Civil Rights Rhetoric, and the Ambivalent Politics of Christian Evangelicalism in New York City." *Sexualities* 16 (3–4): 245–260.

Hefling, Charles, and Cynthia L. Shattuck. (2006). *The Oxford Guide to the Book of Common Prayer: A Worldwide Survey.* New York: Oxford University Press.

Robinson, Gene. (2013). *God Believes in Love: Straight Talk about Gay Marriage.* New York: Vintage.

Shattuck, Gardiner H. (2000). *Episcopalians and Race: Civil War to Civil Rights.* Religion in the South. Lexington: University Press of Kentucky.

Siker, Jeffrey S. (2007). *Homosexuality and Religion: An Encyclopedia.* Westport, CT: Greenwood Press.

Vaughn, J. Barry. (2013). *Bishops, Bourbons, and Big Mules: A History of the Episcopal Church in Alabama.* Religion & American Culture. Tuscaloosa: University of Alabama Press.

# Evangelicals

Unlike some of the other groups outlined in terms of how they view same-sex marriage, evangelicals are not a specific branch of Christianity, nor is there one church that most people think of when they say evangelicals (unlike the Baptists, where most people mean and think Southern Baptists). Instead, *evangelical* refers to a belief system that many churches follow (and others disavow).

The key belief of evangelicals is that one must be born again. While some evangelicals in the 19th century were headed toward reform, most evangelicals after that rejected most, if not all, changes. Most evangelicals aligned themselves with fundamentalists and rejected modern ideas. The branding of people as evangelicals was largely self-chosen and happened in the 1950s. Billy Graham was one of the leading people who proclaimed himself an evangelical, hoping in part to move away from the fundamentalist label. Evangelicals were a large bloc of the Moral Majority and helped Ronald Reagan seize control of the Republican Party and the presidency.

In terms of same-sex attraction, most fundamentalists are strongly opposed to it. Other than this issue, some of the larger concerns that evangelicals fight against are secularism, modernity, and evolution. Many evangelicals want to leave society where it was whenever it last worked for them, and this means having same-sex attraction not exist. In turn, this also means that they oppose same-sex marriage, though most evangelicals stop at same-sex relationships and never bother to consider whether any recognition should be given to any same-sex union, never mind allowing a same-sex marriage. These beliefs are tied into the infallibility of the Bible and a reading of the Bible that does not allow same-sex attraction.

The main reasons that evangelicals oppose same-sex relationships include opposition to elites and the belief that the United States needs to remain Christian. Evangelicals hold that an "elite" is driving a secular agenda and that most Americans do not want it and want to remain Christian. The whole idea that a powerful minority is subverting what the majority wants has been trotted out many times in the United States, and this was no different. (It should be noted that when evangelicals were later confronted with polls that showed most Americans support same-sex marriage, they turned against the idea of majority rule and argued for their version of morality.) The third reason that gay and lesbian people have been opposed is tied in with the whole idea of morality. Same-sex attraction in any form is viewed as immoral, and most evangelicals are in favor of their idea of morality. They argue that same-sex attraction did not used to exist, and so if modernization would cease, same-sex attraction would cease too, improving morality.

More modern opposition comes from people who think that gay people want to rewrite the Bible or remove it and so consider themselves above God or better than God. Rewriting God's idea of marriage as being between a man and a woman is also opposed, obviously. In general, whatever the Bible says goes in the areas of marriage and sexuality and should never be changed.

This group has one of the highest levels of disapproval of same-sex marriage. "Strong disapproval of homosexuality can be found within pockets of the population; one such pocket is the evangelical community. When compared to the general population, over twice the percentage of evangelical Protestants oppose any legal recognition of homosexual unions (65 percent)" (Campbell and Munson 2008, 404). This group will also be hard to convince that same-sex marriage is acceptable, as things noted in the Bible, according to them, should never be changed, allowing for little movement.

It should also be noted that contact with gay people, even those in same-sex marriages, will likely do little to change beliefs. It may change other people's beliefs and might change evangelical beliefs in other areas, but not in the area of gay people and same-sex marriage. The reason for this change is that when people are exposed to a group that they do not know and then see that the group is generally acceptable, the prejudice decreases. However, this generally does not occur for evangelicals in regard to gay people. Ashley A. Baker, and Sarah Brauner-Otto wrote, "In particular, because of the lack of support of evangelical religious authority, law, and custom for homosexuality (or because of the support for anti-homosexual sentiments), social contact may have less influence on beliefs and attitudes about homosexuality among Christian evangelicals than among non-evangelicals" (Baker and Brauner-Otto 2015, 245). Thus, evangelicals may not change that much in the future.

Those who have evangelical beliefs and those who are grouped (or who group themselves) into the evangelical system generally believe that same-sex attraction is a sin and oppose the idea of same-sex marriage. This belief largely comes from the idea that same-sex attraction is banned in the Bible. There is also opposition to secularization and modernization, and many evangelicals see both same-sex attraction and acceptance of same-sex relationships, with things like same-sex marriages, as part of both secularization and modernization. Little change is likely to come quickly as most evangelicals believe the Bible, the root of their beliefs, is not open to interpretation.

*See also:* Baptist Church, The; Davis, Kim, and Other Clerks; Generational Differences; Religious Law and Practice in the United States Historically

## Further Reading

Baker, Ashley A., and Sarah Brauner-Otto. (2015). "My Friend Is Gay, but . . . The Effects of Social Contact on Christian Evangelicals' Beliefs about Gays and Lesbians." *Review of Religious Research* 57 (2): 239–268.

Campbell, David E., and J. Quin Monson. (2008). "The Religion Card." *Public Opinion Quarterly* 72 (3): 399–419.

Lindsay, D. Michael. (2007). *Faith in the Halls of Power: How Evangelicals Joined the American Elite*. New York: Oxford University Press.

Peterson, Kurt W., Thomas S. Kidd, and Darren Dochuk. (2014). *American Evangelicalism: George Marsden and the State of American Religious History.* Notre Dame, IN: University of Notre Dame Press.

Priest, Robert J. (2018). "Same-Sex Sexuality, Marriage, and the Seminary Professor: Catholic, Evangelical, and Mainline Protestant." *Interdisciplinary Journal of Research on Religion* 14 (January): 2–45.

Turner, John G. (2008). *Bill Bright & Campus Crusade for Christ: The Renewal of Evangelicalism in Postwar America.* Chapel Hill: University of North Carolina Press.

# G

## Generational Differences

In many ways, the question of public acceptance of same-sex marriage in most religions is one of generations. In the 1960s, Jack Weinberg said not to trust anyone over 30, so the divide based on age is nothing new. However, in the area of same-sex marriage, it is more apparent than in most other areas. This is not to suggest that there are not differences based in religion, as some religions are more tolerant than others. However, even in those religions, there is a pronounced difference based on age.

In the area of marriage, generational divides are nothing new either. In the past, new trends in marriage, such as marriages between different religions or different races, took time to be accepted, and it seems that people who do not directly know of anything different are more willing to accept things being different than they were before they were born. There is also something generational in terms of the fact that people under a certain age are more accepting.

The same seems true of same-sex marriage. In 2011, one study noted, "There is at least a 20-point generation gap between Millennials (age 18 to 29) and seniors (age 65 and older) on every public policy measure in the survey concerning rights for gay and lesbian people" (Jones, Cox, and Cook 2011). In 2019, another survey found a 29 percent difference between the baby boomers and the millennials, which now were defined slightly differently.

Those over 65 were the most resistant. This suggests that the older you are, the more resistant you are to doing things differently. This is reflected in the old saying, "You can't teach an old dog new tricks." This may or may not be true, but the important thing to know is that the older generation will in time become less politically important. With each four-year electoral cycle, a significant number of those over age 65 stop voting. Thus, for future years, what the younger generation thinks is more important.

One question, of course, is whether Generation X and the millennials will change (or continue to change, in the case of Gen X) their views as they age. Most prior generations have become somewhat more conservative and less likely to change as they age. Some research casts doubt on whether millennials will do the same. Of course, with no set definition of the millennial generation, it is difficult to track these views over time. There is also the question of whether a view on same-sex marriage necessarily tracks with conservative or liberal, even if conservative is equated with not wanting change. After all, the millennials have had same-sex marriage (if we define millennials as those born after 1982) in at least some state for most of their adult lives by this point (even for the oldest millennials). Thus, it is not a change to support same-sex marriage, but it would be a change to want it removed.

The reason that this matters for same-sex marriage is that if the generational divide holds true, the overall support for same-sex marriage will increase over time. Thus, if society waits long enough (and the younger generation, or the millennials (and whatever comes after them), supports it more than the older one), marriage equality will be welcomed in. On the other hand, if a certain percentage of opposition will exist regardless of age, those favoring marriage equality still have a significant amount of work to do to convince more of the population.

One might assume that since the policy became law, it would be accepted, but if other policies mandated by the courts are examined, it can be seen that public avoidance or opposition continues. For instance, even though integration was mandated for education in *Brown v. Board of Education* in 1954, vocal public opposition continued until the 1970s, and quiet opposition continued after that. More recent studies have noted that the educational marketplace in many cities, if not nationwide, is now more segregated than it was before *Brown*.

Other examples abound as well. *Roe v. Wade* is probably the most well-known example of a U.S. Supreme Court case that has not set an issue to rest just because the court spoke. While there are multiple differences between marriage equality and abortion (and some similarities), the point here is that when the Supreme Court spoke, the people did not listen (to paraphrase the old E.F. Hutton ads). The same has been true of the Supreme Court, one should remember, ever since it started ruling.

Thus, while generational differences suggest that the public may come to accept marriage equality over time, the issue is far from certain. Those in favor of marriage equality should be hopeful but not certain that the road forward looks promising.

*See also:* Buttigieg, Pete; New Bills Opposing Same-Sex Marriage; Religious Law and Practice in the United States Historically; 2004 Elections and Religion; 2000s, The

## Further Reading

Cohen, Cathy J. (2011). "Millennials & the Myth of the Post-Racial Society: Black Youth, Intra-Generational Divisions & the Continuing Racial Divide in American Politics." *Daedalus* 140 (2): 197.

Jones, Robert P., Daniel Cox, and Elizabeth Cook. (2011). "Generations at Odds: The Millennial Generation and the Future of Gay and Lesbian Rights." PRRI, August 29. http://www.prri.org/research/generations-at-odds/.

Lee, Hye-Yon, and Diana C. Mutz. (2018). "Changing Attitudes toward Same-Sex Marriage: A Three-Wave Panel Study." *Political Behavior* (May) 41: 701–722.

Polikoff, Nancy D. (2008). *Beyond Straight and Gay Marriage: Valuing All Families under the Law*. Boston: Beacon Press.

Rosenfeld, Michael J. (2007). *The Age of Independence: Interracial Unions, Same-Sex Unions, and the Changing American Family*. Cambridge, MA: Harvard University Press.

Turner, Ronald. (2016). "Marriage Equality and Obergefell's Generational (Not Glucksberg's Traditional) Due Process Clause." *Duke Journal of Gender Law & Policy* 2: 145.

## Governmental Benefits

This entry looks at the governmental benefits of marriage and how those are either given easily to same-sex married couples or only reluctantly given. It also looks at marriage and examines how marriage means so much more than just a title. It should be noted that the rights given to a married couple vary country by country. Also, not all countries treat the rights of same-sex married couples the same. This entry looks mostly at the United States.

In the United States, the rights given to married couples are numerous. Those include economic rights, inheritance rights, rights in court, and death benefits. One economic right is the ability to open a banking account together. One inheritance right is the right to inherit property. Very often, a tax break comes to a spouse that might not come to another person. There are also rights in court. One generally cannot be forced to testify against one's spouse. In terms of death benefits, most states automatically grant property to one's spouse, particularly if no other provisions have been made in a will.

It should be noted that most governmental bills allow third parties to discriminate, rather than allowing the government itself to discriminate. Quite a few states have "religious freedom" bills that allow adoption agencies or counselors to discriminate on the basis of sexual orientation or a same-sex marriage. Many of these states do not have a general antidiscrimination law, so this is not an exemption to the general policy being carved out as much as it is a license to discriminate.

Many governments hire at least in part based on a set of unspoken qualifications that compare candidates and look for the "best fit." This allows a license to discriminate in employment, at least at some level. The U.S. Supreme Court has also not ruled that sexual orientation cannot be used to discriminate, which means that the governmental benefit of being able to find a job is not available for those in same-sex marriages in some states.

Some governmental benefits have improved for those in same-sex marriage and for those who believe in equality in recent years. For instance, a number of states have acted to ban "conversion therapy," which aims to brainwash people into not being gay. Other states have acted to increase protections for same-sex couples specifically and for LGBTQ people in general.

Some Native American tribes do not allow same-sex marriage, and so these tribes do not give any benefits to same-sex couples. This can be important if the tribe is gaining significant revenue from gambling (as some tribes are) and using this revenue to give a better benefit to those who are married. It should be noted that only some Native American tribes and the American Samoa territory do not allow same-sex marriage in the United States.

Thus, same-sex marriage is allowed in nearly all parts of the United States, and governments are generally supposed to treat it the same as opposite-sex marriage. However, governments do sometimes promote policies that allow entities that perform governmental functions, such as administering adoptions, to discriminate.

*See also:* Adoption; Davis, Kim, and Other Clerks; Defense of Marriage Act, The; *Masterpiece Cakeshop v. Colorado Civil Rights Commission*; Religious Freedom Restoration Act

## Further Reading

Higdon, Michael J. (2019). "Biological Citizenship and the Children of Same-Sex Marriage." *George Washington Law Review* 87 (1): 124.

Malta, Monica, Reynaldo Cardoso, Luiz Montenegro, Jaqueline Gomes de Jesus, Michele Seixas, Bruna Benevides, Maria das Dores Silva, Sara LeGrand, and Kathryn Whetten. (2019). "Sexual and Gender Minorities Rights in Latin America and the Caribbean: A Multi-Country Evaluation." *BMC International Health and Human Rights* 19 (1): 31.

Mayeri, Serena. (2015). "Marital Supremacy and the Constitution of the Nonmarital Family." *California Law Review* 103 (5): 1277–1352.

McEvoy, J. P. (1994). "The Charter and Spousal Benefits: The Case of the Same-Sex Spouse." *Review of Constitutional Studies* 1: 39.

Sunstein, Cass R. (2004). "The Right to Marry." *Cardozo Law Review* 26 (2081). https://chicagounbound.uchicago.edu/cgi/viewcontent.cgi?article=12501& context=journal_articles.

# H

## History and Religion

History and religion are important topics to consider when dealing with same-sex marriage. At first blush, history would seem to favor those opposed to same-sex marriage. After all, no country in the world allowed same-sex marriage until 2000, at least in modern years, and no religion generally allowed it until the Quakers did so in the 1980s. Some have even used that seemingly solid block to suggest that because it was never allowed in the past, it should not be allowed now.

However, such marriages have occurred in the past. One Roman emperor, around 50 CE, married at least two men. As the Roman emperors considered themselves to be gods, this was an interesting mix of religion and same-sex marriage. One might argue that the Romans were no one to be copied, but it at least proves that it did happen. Same-sex marriages also sometimes occurred in other cultures as well. Some religions allowed legal occurrences of things that provided for some of the same benefits as marriage under another name. In the Middle Ages, *brotherment* occurred, where two people agreed to share one house and one income and lived much the same as man and wife. Some of these were probably financial, but others were not. As most European countries had a union of church and state, religion allowed these arrangements to occur.

In other periods, some couples moving toward marriage were found to be of the same sex. In France, in the 1700s, priests noted that they questioned a number of couples who were of the same sex. Some of them found other priests who would marry them. This all points to people of the same sex being married, even though it was not legal. In other cultures, a marriage license was not always demanded of couples who claimed to be married. This allowed same-sex couples to pose as opposite-sex couples and act as if they were married, even when they were not. Without adequate records, it is difficult to profile small towns, which is where most lived before the modern era.

In early American history, some cases of lesbian couples existed. In one example, two women lived in the same household, owned a business together, and presented themselves as a married couple to the town in which they lived. They did not seek the sanction of the state and were accepted into the church where they worshipped. One of the women was even a deacon and so was a leader in her church.

On the American frontier, there was a fair amount of distance, and so it can be expected that at least some same-sex couples pretended to be of the opposite sex and even married. These were often not discovered. One soldier's wife on a western outpost after the Civil War was found to be a man when the wife died unexpectedly while the soldier was off on a patrol. The local women went to dress the body for burial and found the wife to be a man. Women also sometimes dressed as men and fought in the Civil War, so some remaining as men afterward would not be unexpected. Cross-dressing and cross-living probably went both ways. The number of people living as the opposite sex to live with the one they loved cannot be evaluated, as only the discovered cases would have made it into the popular press.

Once cities grew up, many women craved the freedom to live on their own. Few places would rent to single women, and so many women shared houses, sometimes in pairs. Some of these shared living quarters were sexual, and some were not. These were often called "Boston marriages," named after Henry James's novel *The Bostonians*, which discussed two such women living together. James did not use that term, but others combined the practice and the book title and described it as such. One such pair of women was Annie Adams Fields and Sarah Orne Jewett. Their relationship is unclear in terms of whether it was sexual. One such 19th-century pairing that most people believe to have been sexual was Willa Cather and Edith Lewis, who were buried together in the same grave. That strongly suggests that it was more than just a convenience or that they were living together just to give each woman more freedom.

There were also some well-known 19th-century long-term pairs of men. Some of these were even connected to religious events and religions. These included Walt Whitman and Peter Doyle. Probably a higher percentage of men who lived together had sexual relationships, as men could live on their own, which removes that reason for living together. Sexual attitudes also have greatly changed since the 19th century, and so it is very difficult to read today's issues into the past.

While not related to same-sex marriage, history and religion both informed the interracial marriage debate. After the end of slavery (directly related to both religion and history), Southern states controlled by whites (and some Northern and Western states) banned marriage between races. Some only banned marriages between whites and Blacks, and others banned marriages between whites and nonwhites. Few banned marriages between races in general (in other words, any nonwhite was always allowed to marry any other nonwhite, regardless of their race).

***See also:*** AIDS; *Loving v. Virginia*; Religion and Interracial Marriage; Religious Law and Practice in the United States Historically; 2000s, The

## Further Reading

Blanton, DeAnne, and Lauren M. Cook. (2003). *They Fought like Demons: Women Soldiers in the American Civil War*. First Vintage Civil War Library ed. New York: Vintage Civil War Library.

Cleves, Rachel Hope. (2014). *Charity and Sylvia: A Same-Sex Marriage in Early America*. New York: Oxford University Press.

D'Emilio, John, and Estelle B. Freedman. (2012). *Intimate Matters: A History of Sexuality in America*. 3rd ed. Chicago: University of Chicago Press.

James, Henry. (2014). *The Bostonians*. New York: Heritage Illustrated Publishing.

Stevens, Julie Anne. (2018). *Two Irish Girls in Bohemia: The Drawings and Writings of E. E. Somerville and Martin Ross*. West Cork (IE): Somerville Press.

# Islam

The Islamic faith, while presented as monolithic in the Western media, is really incredibly varied. However, the views of only the two main branches of that faith will be presented here, Shia and Sunni, and even within those branches of the faith, there is variation as well. It should be noted that many Islamic states exist, and some of those states will be included. However, the view of any state that claims to be Islamic is not always the same as the people of the Islamic faith.

The Shia branch of Islam (the branches are presented alphabetically) holds that only the descendants of Muhammad, the founder of Islam, deserve to lead it. It is also sometimes called Shiite (and the followers are called Shias and Shiites), with the varying spelling in part due to transliteration from Arabic. One of the main countries that is Shia is Iran. Iran bans gay people, holding that being gay is one of the worst things that can be done. One of Iran's religious leaders said, "There is no worst form of moral degeneration than homosexuality" (OutRight Action International 2016).

Some countries have gone beyond just condemning it and allowed murder. This was the case in Chechnya, an area in Russia that is overwhelmingly Sunni Muslim. In Chechnya, the government has aimed to drive all gay people out of the area. The government of the area denies repression but also offers an interesting justification for not needing the repression. One government leader argued that there was no need for any government repression as there were no gay people in Chechnya (he did not say how they figured that out). If there were, he added, their families would have killed them.

The Sunni branch of Islam holds that Ali, the son-in-law of Muhammad, was not the rightful successor. Sunnis are the largest group in several

Muslim-majority countries, including Egypt, Turkey, and Syria. In none of those countries, though, does a religious faction drive the government, unlike in Iran. Overall, Sunni is the largest branch in the world.

While most people in Saudi Arabia are Sunni, the government is driven by a branch of Islam called Salafi, which is a much stricter interpretation of Sunni Islam than most. In Saudi Arabia, being gay or lesbian can lead to a public whipping or other penalties, up to being imprisoned for life. Being caught in a same-sex sexual act can lead to capital punishment. Needless to say, Saudi Arabia does not allow for same-sex marriage. In 2013, Saudi Arabia even considered making an effort to ban gay foreigners from entering the country: "Gulf nations may soon conduct tests to 'detect' gays traveling to those nations in order to deny them entry" (Sieczkowski 2013).

One government that is Sunni and that allows the religion to have great influence is Azerbaijan. It allows same-sex activity but gives no form of recognition for same-sex couples. There is no legality to any same-sex union. In some estimates, Azerbaijan provides the least protection of any European country.

Neither the Shia nor Sunni branch is monolithic, although the view of most Islamic religious figures on same-sex attraction is a very negative one. They are also not the only Islamic branches, just the ones most publicly recognized. This does not aim to suggest that there are not people who are gay or lesbian and Islamic, as there surely are. They are just not supported, generally, by their religion, especially the larger structures. This entry also does not aim to suggest that there are no Muslims in the United States who are tolerant of gay people, whether they are Islamic or of another religion. It just aims to suggest that these groups are not given much press, and, based on their religion, they may not want whatever press they might be given for being tolerant.

*See also:* Catholic Church, The; Eastern Orthodox Church, The; History and Religion; Judaism; Same-Sex Marriage Worldwide

## Further Reading

El-Rouayheb, Khaled. (2005). *Before Homosexuality in the Arab-Islamic World, 1500–1800.* Chicago: University of Chicago Press.

Habib, Samar. (2010). *Islam and Homosexuality.* Westport, CT: Praeger.

OutRight Action International. (2016). "Iran's Supreme Leader Says There's No Worse Form of Moral Degeneration Than Homosexuality." OutRight Action

International, May 27, 2016. https://outrightinternational.org/content/irans-supreme-leader-says-there-no-worst-form-moral-degeneration-homosexuality.

Sardar, Ziauddin. (2011). *Reading the Qur'an: The Contemporary Relevance of the Sacred Text of Islam*. New York: Oxford University Press.

Sieczkowski, Cavan. (2013). "Gulf Countries Propose Test to 'Detect' Gays, Ban Them from Entering." HuffPost, October 9, 2013. https://www.huffpost.com/entry/gulf-countries-detect-gays_n_4065927.

Siker, Jeffrey S. (2007). *Homosexuality and Religion: An Encyclopedia*. Westport, CT: Greenwood Press.

Wuthnow, Robert. (2007). *Encyclopedia of Politics and Religion*. Washington, DC: CQ Press.

# J

## Judaism

Judaism started roughly 6,000 years ago. Jews believe that God, who created the world, gave them a unique covenant. Today, Judaism has at least four branches, and their views on same-sex attraction and same-sex marriage will be surveyed in this entry. Across the entire world, Judaism has between 10 million and 20 million adherents, putting it in the top ten of all religions.

The oldest religious branch of Judaism is Orthodox Judaism. Orthodox Judaism is also the official state religion of the State of Israel. This branch holds that the Torah should be followed word for word for each requirement. There are over 600 rules to be followed. Orthodox Judaism largely aims to keep the religion the same way it was (as far as they are concerned) in the time that it was founded. The Orthodox branch largely opposes same-sex attraction, and so it should not be surprising that it opposes same-sex marriage as well.

Orthodox Judaism is a very male-centered religion. Only men may be leaders, and the men are separated from the women during worship services. However, even within this religion and within Israel, where the Orthodox religion is the state religion, religious traditions can be used to build connections. Lustenberger contends, "It is not surprising that many lesbian women and gay men have developed antagonistic feelings toward Orthodox authorities. However, this does not mean that they unilaterally rebuff Jewish traditions. . . . I argue quite the opposite—that the significance of Jewish lifecycle rituals for same-sex couples cannot be underestimated" (Lustenberger 2013, 141).

A second branch of Judaism is Conservative Judaism (which now is in the middle of the Judaic religious spectrum, despite the name). Conservative Judaism started in the late 1800s. Unlike Orthodox Judaism's view that the

Torah is infallible and that God gave the law, Conservative Judaism allows for the role of people, and there is a lot of research into the history involved. Conservative Judaism moved in the mid- and late 20th century to admit women fully into the faith, starting with integrated seating of both sexes.

In terms of same-sex attraction, Conservative Judaism calls for inclusion and acceptance. In the area of same-sex marriage, the overall branch allows it, but it is up to each synagogue. For all Jewish marriages in the Conservative branch, the marriage must also be between two Jews. As noted, though, this is not discrimination against same-sex marriages. When the Conservative branch allowed same-sex marriages, there was very little reaction in the branch: "The Conservative Jewish movement established guidelines in early June for the marriage of gay and lesbian couples. The reaction so far? Hard to find" (Markoe 2012, 19).

A third branch of Judaism is Reform Judaism (these branches have been presented across the spectrum of Judaism, not by the age of the branch). Reform Judaism started in the early 1800s. It aimed to reach out to modern people and was a response both to the times and to Orthodox Judaism (Reform preceded Conservative). The movement was biggest in Germany and the United States, and reforms happened more quickly in the United States, with people sitting by families in services and divorce in the civil courts with no involvement of the rabbi being required.

In terms of same-sex attraction, Reform Judaism today embraces the LGBTQ community, holding that God made people and so God made everyone. They also say that all people who have been discriminated against should hold together. Reform Judaism also welcomes same-sex couples and performs same-sex marriage, having supported those ceremonies since 2000, before any U.S. state allowed them.

The final branch is Reconstructionist Judaism. It is the most liberal branch and the furthest away from Orthodox Judaism (the Orthodox branch considers it to not be true Judaism). It holds that Jewish law, as a whole, is neither divinely inspired nor regulating, but it should be followed unless there is a reason for a change. Unlike the other branches, it allows non-Jews to fully participate and is moving toward allowing rabbis to have non-Jewish partners, on a synagogue-by-synagogue basis. It allows rabbis to be LGBTQ. Not surprisingly, it also allows for same-sex marriages. Overall, Reconstructionist Judaism is the smallest of the four branches.

This is not an exhaustive list, and Judaism is ever changing, particularly in the modern period. With access to the internet, a lot of splinter groups of all religions (not just Judaism by any means) can link up and form a larger movement. This gives them staying power as well as increased visibility. However, in the area of same-sex marriage, the four branches listed above are the most viable in the United States. It should also be noted that the movement of three of the four branches toward allowing same-sex marriages and rabbis to officiate in same-sex marriages did not cause as much of a stir as in other denominations. Perhaps that is something that the United States as a whole could learn from.

*See also:* Baptist Church, The; Catholic Church, The; Islam; Methodists; Same-Sex Marriage Worldwide

## Further Reading

Biale, David. (2011). *Not in the Heavens: The Tradition of Jewish Secular Thought*. Princeton, NJ: Princeton University Press.

Goodman, Martin. (2018). *A History of Judaism*. Princeton, NJ: Princeton University Press.

Jordan, Mark D., Meghan T. Sweeney, and David M. Mellott. (2006). *Authorizing Marriage: Canon, Tradition, and Critique in the Blessing of Same-Sex Unions*. Princeton, NJ: Princeton University Press.

Levenson, Alan T. (2012). *The Wiley-Blackwell History of Jews and Judaism*. The Wiley-Blackwell Histories of Religion. Hoboken, NJ: Wiley-Blackwell.

Lustenberger, Sibylle. (2013). "Conceiving Judaism: The Challenges of Same-Sex Parenthood." *Israel Studies Review* 28 (2): 140–156.

Markoe, Lauren. (2012). "Conservative Jews' Shift on Gay Rites Causes No Stir." *Christian Century* 14: 19.

Neusner, Jacob. (2011). *The Transformation of Judaism: From Philosophy to Religion*. Studies in Judaism. Lanham, MD: University Press of America.

# L

## *Loving v. Virginia*

The *Loving v. Virginia* decision in 1967 dealt with the question of marriage equality and being allowed to choose who we love, similar to the 2015 *Obergefell* decision. However, *Loving* dealt with marriage equality between different races as opposed to the issue of same-sex marriage in *Obergefell*. One similarity, though, is that religion was used in both cases to deny marriage equality.

In 1924, Virginia passed a Racial Integrity Act with the initial aim of preventing interracial marriage between Black and white Americans and strengthening a ban that already existed. However, its main effect was to ban anyone who had nonwhite ancestors from marrying anyone whose ancestry was determined to be wholly white. Religion was not a stated part of the issue, but it absolutely played a role. White supremacists used religion as a tool to enforce all kinds of Jim Crow laws, and the white voting public in Virginia generally accepted the goals of such groups as the Ku Klux Klan.

Most churches were only one race by default, and religion had been used to defend slavery in multiple ways. One of the most popular arguments favoring slavery and, by extension after the Civil War, segregation was connected to the "Curse of Ham." Ham was one of the three sons of Noah. As a result of seeing his father naked, Ham was cursed by Noah and made a servant of the other two sons. "American Bible readers interpreted this story of 'Noah's curse' and the dispersion of Noah's sons as a justification and explanation for racial slavery" (Botham 2009, 94). A second common view was that slavery was justified in the Bible, as one Bible verse has slaves being told to obey their masters.

It should also be noted that the law in question in *Loving v. Virginia* did not originate until 1924. Thus, while it may be seen as a product of the late

19th century, there were still new concerns in the early 20th century. The result was also in large part the product of one man, Walter Plecker, who in turn was Virginia's first registrar in the Bureau of Vital Statistics. These bureaus across the country were a product of the Progressive Era and the desire to compile and record these statistics and use them to improve the country. Plecker thought that many Blacks had "fooled their marital partners, eluded the scrutiny of county officials, or lulled or threatened their neighbors into recognizing them as 'white'" (Pascoe 2009, 141).

Virginia had an interracial marriage ban, but that only prevented people with one-quarter African American blood from marrying whites. Plecker wanted a total ban. The total ban, though, was politically unworkable, as many Virginians were quite proud to claim heritage from Native Americans. By the time the ban was adopted, those with one-sixteenth of Native American blood (or one great-great-grandfather) were allowed to marry whites, and the registration was only voluntary. The religious element was not heavily emphasized. Plecker was focused more on the "Anglo-Saxon" heritage, but many at the time had turned *Anglo-Saxon* into *WASP* (white Anglo-Saxon Protestant) in their minds. This is somewhat similar to early bans on same-sex marriage being just understood rather than specifically spelled out with justifications.

The ban on interracial marriage was not formally challenged in federal court until the 1960s. State court challenges were seen as futile, and the U.S. Supreme Court wanted to duck the issue. Even while squarely faced with the issue, it declined. The NAACP also had little interest in the 1950s, holding it to be too soon after *Brown v. Board of Education*. In 1962, the case of *McLaughlin v. Florida* came in front of the U.S. Supreme Court. This case struck down the 1882 *Pace* case, which had criminalized interracial cohabitation, but did not overturn interracial marriage bans; it just stated that Florida's justification was not strong enough. This was important, as all of the previous cases heard in the lower courts had relied on *Pace* as a straightforward way of upholding the interracial marriage bans.

*Loving v. Virginia* arose out of both the time and place. The 1960s were seen as the start of the civil rights era in many people's minds. This is not to project what came later in the mid and late 1960s into the early 1960s but more to note that many people were ready for the civil rights revolution, and John Kennedy's rhetoric was more encouraging of that movement (even if he was not) than Eisenhower.

Mildred Jeter married Richard Loving in 1958, and they were quickly arrested in Virginia. After they were convicted and sentenced to a one-year sentence, they were allowed to leave the state if they agreed not to return together. In 1964, while living in Washington, DC, they wrote Attorney General Robert Kennedy and asked for help in returning to Virginia. Kennedy directed them to the American Civil Liberties Union (ACLU). The ACLU asked the state court to vacate the sentence, but it was upheld, with the judge ruling that "Almighty God created the races white, black, yellow, malay and red, and he placed them on separate continents. And but for the interference with his arrangement there would be no cause for such marriages. The fact that he separated the races shows that he did not intend for the races to mix" ("Opinion of Judge Leon M. Bazile" 2014).

Their case was heard by the U.S. Supreme Court in 1967. The Supreme Court, in a 9–0 ruling, struck down the ban as a violation of the equal protection clause and the due process clause and held that one has a fundamental right to marry. This eventually impacted the same-sex marriage issue; if one has a fundamental right to marry, then couples should be able to marry regardless of their sexual orientation. Most fundamental rights can only be restricted under extraordinary circumstances, especially if the restriction is a general one. Indeed, when marriage equality was announced in the *Obergefell* decision, the right to marry was one of the bases that the decision used.

*See also:* Chalcedon Movement; Defense of Marriage Act, The; *Obergefell v. Hodges*; Religion and Interracial Marriage; Religious Law and Practice in the United States Historically

## Further Reading

Botham, Fay. (2009). *Almighty God Created the Races: Christianity, Interracial Marriage & American Law*. Chapel Hill: University of North Carolina Press.

Newbeck, Phyl. (2008). *Virginia Hasn't Always Been for Lovers: Interracial Marriage Bans and the Case of Richard and Mildred Loving*. Carbondale: Southern Illinois University Press.

Nobel Maillard, Kevin. (2012). Loving v. Virginia *in a Post-Racial World: Rethinking Race, Sex, and Marriage*. Cambridge, UK: Cambridge University Press.

"Opinion of Judge Leon M. Bazile." (2014). Encyclopedia of Virginia. https://encyclopediavirginia.org/entries/judgment-against-richard-and-mildred-loving-january-6-1959/#content.

Pascoe, Peggy. (2009). *What Comes Naturally: Miscegenation Law and the Making of Race in America*. New York: Oxford University Press.

Wallenstein, Peter. (2002). *Tell the Court I Love My Wife: Race, Marriage, and Law: An American History*. New York: Palgrave Macmillan.

# M

## *Masterpiece Cakeshop* v. *Colorado Civil Rights Commission*

The *Masterpiece Cakeshop* case made news because it dealt with the clash of two constitutionally protected freedoms: one person's freedom of religion, in the area of free exercise, and another person's right to equality.

This case occurred in Colorado after another state had ruled in favor of same-sex marriage before Colorado. However, Colorado did have a statute prohibiting the different treatment of people on the basis of sexual orientation. A couple had traveled to Massachusetts to be married and then returned to Colorado. They then wanted a cake produced for a celebration. The cake shop refused (it should be noted that the cake shop would allow them to buy other things, but not a wedding cake, and that nothing about the wedding cake was discussed). The couple then filed a complaint with the commission, which ruled against the cake shop. It should be noted that Colorado's antidiscrimination ordinance specifically prohibited discrimination on the basis of sexual orientation. The cake shop's defense was that the creation of a custom cake was an endorsement of the message of the couple's wedding. The commission held that creating cakes was an expected part of the cake shop's business, and so the failure to do so was discrimination.

The Colorado Supreme Court refused to hear the case, and it was appealed to the U.S. Supreme Court. At the Supreme Court, issues of free speech and freedom of religion were considered. The issue of free speech was included because making a product is sometimes considered expressive speech. The ruling from the Supreme Court was relatively narrow and focused on the conduct of the Colorado Civil Rights Commission.

This was not the first case heard, even on cakes, by the Colorado Civil Rights Commission, and this mattered to the court. In a previous case, the commission had allowed three bakeries to refuse to make a cake with an antigay Bible quote. The commission tried to say that since the other bakeries had made Christian cakes for others, this was allowable discrimination based on the message that was being printed, not banned discrimination based on religion. The Supreme Court chose to focus on this differential treatment rather than focusing on the main issue presented by the case. The Trump administration chose to support the cake shop rather than supporting the Colorado Civil Rights Commission.

It should be noted that religiously based conduct that discriminates was not new with this case. One of the reasons that the state district court gave in the *Loving* decision (dealing with interracial marriage) was that God did not want interracial marriage. In that case, the Supreme Court disagreed. Other cases have also had people claim religious justification for discrimination.

The Supreme Court's narrow 7–2 decision overturned the commission's ruling. The main opinion was written by Justice Kennedy. Kennedy noted the language of the commission, as it had paralleled the cake shop's owner's belief to that of someone who had defended the Holocaust, and Kennedy viewed this as hostility to religion. He also said that the commission's treatment of the cake shop owner's religion was not parallel to what it had done to the person who did not want to bake the cake with the antigay verse. (It was not mentioned in Kennedy's opinion that the couple had left before discussing any specifics of the cake.)

There were also two concurrences filed and one dissent. One of the concurrences, by Justice Kagan, noted how narrow the decision was, and another, by Justice Thomas, noted that the issues of free speech and the free exercise of religion were not ruled upon. Thomas's opinion made clear that he would have ruled for the cake shop had those two things been considered. The dissent, by Justice Ginsburg, stated that the commission should have been upheld and that the commission was right to rule the way it did, as the denial by the cake shop was based on a protected trait, and such discrimination was illegal.

The *Masterpiece Cakeshop* case ended, but neither the issue nor the bakery was in the clear. The issue was not over, not even in terms of cases in the legal pipeline when the *Masterpiece Cakeshop* case was decided. In 2017, the cake shop refused to bake a cake for a transgender woman who wanted to honor her change of gender. The case was then taken to the Colorado Civil Rights Commission, and the cake shop countersued. The case was dropped in 2019, and the individual then sued the cake shop. The issue overall was also not dead; a flower shop had been fined, and the case was sent back to the lower courts after the *Masterpiece* decision. The ruling against the flower shop was upheld, but the case is still in the courts as of the writing of this book. There are also cases against cake shops and photographers working through the courts. Thus, *Masterpiece Cakeshop* dodged the issue of whether religiously based conduct that discriminates is allowable, and the issue continues.

*See also:* Defense of Marriage Act, The; *Loving v. Virginia*; *Obergefell v. Hodges*; Religious Freedom Restoration Act; Restaurants

## Further Reading

Miller, Brian K. (2018). "Reconciling Religious Freedom and LGBT Rights: The Perils and Promises of Masterpiece Cakeshop." *George Mason University Civil Rights Law Journal* 3: 245.

Movsesian, Mark L. (2019). "*Masterpiece Cakeshop* and the Future of Religious Freedom." *Harvard Journal of Law & Public Policy* 42 (3): 711–750.

Schoen, Edward J. (2019). "Masterpiece Cakeshop: A Case Study Brought to You by the U.S. Supreme Court." *Southern Law Journal* 29 (1): 25–68.

Smith, Miriam Catherine. (2008). *Political Institutions and Lesbian and Gay Rights in the United States and Canada*. Routledge Studies in North American Politics. New York: Routledge.

Turk, Katherine. (2016). *Equality on Trial: Gender and Rights in the Modern American Workplace*. Politics and Culture in Modern America. Philadelphia: University of Pennsylvania Press.

# Mennonites

While same-sex marriage is very modern and most Mennonite and associated faiths are viewed as not being overly modern, it is still important to consider this group for several reasons. The first is that the Mennonites and other groups may be seen as dated, but they are actually making somewhat of a resurgence. Part of the reason for this is that they are successful, and another reason is that they provide a support structure that is often lacking in today's society. Thus, this group is not fading away. It should also be noted that a wide variety of groups is being considered here. This entry covers the Mennonites, the Amish, and the Hutterites, who are all collectively part of the Anabaptists. They are also not a small group, or a small collection, in terms of population when viewed together. The Anabaptists as a whole are about two million people, with about one million of those being in the United States. While that may seem like a small number, it is more than the number of people who live in several states with populations of less than one million.

The Mennonites are more modern than some of the other Anabaptists, especially in terms of their use of technology. Many Mennonites use electricity (the lack of which is one of the more distinctive things most people associate with the Amish), but they often still live in their own communities. Another thing that marks Mennonites as being different from the majority of the country is a commitment to pacifism. Mennonites, in the area of LGBTQ equality, have been more open than some more traditional religions. Some groups of the Mennonite have argued for full inclusion, and the Mennonite Church USA has allowed LGBTQ people to become ministers. There have also been some Mennonite ministers who have officiated (and were allowed to officiate) at same-sex weddings since 2015. Some conferences, though, have chosen to leave the Mennonite Church USA, feeling that it has become too liberal.

The Amish are the Anabaptists that get the most publicity. They are known for their cooking and crafts, much more so than the other groups. They are also most noted for staying away from society and their lack of use of electricity. (It should be noted that, similar to the Mennonites, there is a range of behavior among those who consider themselves Amish. A small fraction, probably about 10%, do use electricity, similar to the fraction of Mennonites who do not use electricity.)

The Amish view same-sex attraction as a sin, and it also goes against their whole family structure. The Amish want people to marry other Amish and have large families in a system that does not use technology. On just a practical level, someone who is attracted to the same sex is less likely to have a large family. The Amish also follow their interpretation of the Bible, which holds that same-sex attraction is a sin. One might wonder what being Amish and gay means, but it varies depending on who you talk to—the Amish group or the LGBTQ child. The Amish group claims that there are no gay people in the population, while the LGBTQ child generally wants to grow up and leave the group. Both groups are unlikely to talk about the issue while the child is still in the population. The Amish also shun publicity and so would be unlikely to cover the issue.

The Hutterites are the third-largest Anabaptist group in the United States, although they receive even less press than the Mennonites. They are also probably the smallest group in the United States of these three. The Hutterites live collectively and own everything in common. The community divides up the work. Technology use is allowed in business but generally shunned in one's personal life. The Hutterites generally oppose same-sex attraction. They view it as a sin, and so, not surprisingly, they also oppose same-sex marriage. Generally, the Hutterites do not take political stands (or get involved in court), so it should not be surprising that this view is not as public as you might expect. With the community lifestyle, there is probably less disagreement voiced than there would be in one connected with the larger world.

The Anabaptists have a wide variety of groups under their umbrella, and all have somewhat unique lifestyles. They also have a wide variety of views on how LGBTQ people should be treated. The Mennonites generally allow equality, the Amish claim that it does not exist, and the Hutterites view it as sin. There is, of course, probably a wide variety of views in each local community, but with these groups shut away from the world, it is probably studied less than in other religious groups.

*See also:* Generational Differences; Mormons; Pentecostals; Religious Law and Practice in the United States Historically

## Further Reading

Camden, Laura L., and Susan Gaetz Duarte. (2006). *Mennonites in Texas: The Quiet in the Land.* Sam Rayburn Series on Rural Life: No. 12. College Station: Texas A & M University Press.

Hauerwas, Stanley, and Samuel Wells. (2011). *The Blackwell Companion to Christian Ethics.* Blackwell Companions to Religion. New York: Wiley-Blackwell.

Hershberger, Anne Krabill. (1999). *Sexuality: God's Gift.* Arlington, VA: Herald Press.

Hillstrom, Kevin. (2008). *Religion and Sexuality.* Opposing Viewpoints in Context. Farmington Hills, MI: Greenhaven Press.

Kraybill, Donald B., and James P. Hurd. (2006). *Horse-and-Buggy Mennonites: Hoofbeats of Humility in a Postmodern World.* Pennsylvania German History and Culture Series. University Park: Pennsylvania State University Press.

# Methodists

The main branch of the Methodist Church in the United States is the United Methodist Church, and it has about seven million U.S. members.

This is the main branch discussed in this entry, although there will also be some offshoots. The United Methodist Church (UMC), by that name, is somewhat new, being founded in 1968, but its roots go back to the 18th century. The Methodist Church split in the United States in the 19th century over slavery but then reunited, mostly, in 1968. The African Methodist Episcopal Church (AME) is primarily an African American religion and is not dealt with here, but it should be noted that there are about a million or more AME members in the United States, with two to three million worldwide.

The Methodist Church is run by bishops, and the bishop of a certain area sets the policy for the area and generally assigns ministers. Most Methodist ministers also move around at set junctures. Local congregations can have input (and definitely can remove ministers), but the bishop generally assigns them. Policy in the UMC is directed at the international level, with the International United Methodist Church setting the overall policy.

The UMC has generally had a strong stand against same-sex attraction, but there are growing fissures within the church. The policy is set by the General Conference, which represents the whole world. In 2019, the delegates from Africa and Asia united with some U.S. delegates to continue a ban on same-sex marriages and also to ban LGBTQ clergy. It went further, though, and put in some strong penalties for those who do not follow the church guidelines. Many in the United States do not agree, and some are calling for leaving the Methodist Church. This would not be unprecedented (the split), as there was previously a split over slavery, and some of the churches who did not like the 1968 merger split off before the two main Methodist churches reunited into the UMC.

The dissension has now spread down to the more local conferences, and part of the disagreement is over what level of welcome a church should give to LGBTQ people if they are not allowed to be clergy or have weddings. Those who view LGBTQ behavior as wrong say that they are treating LGBTQ people the same as any other group that sins, but LGBTQ people, not surprisingly, view that as hate. Some of the local conferences passed resolutions condemning the behavior of the General Conference, a step that does not bode well for long-term peace in the conference. In other conferences, bishops have ordained LGBTQ clergy, holding that this was the right thing to do.

In 2020, another general conference was supposed to meet, but coronavirus postponed that. The next meeting has been scheduled for 2022. If the policy holds, one would expect more Methodist churches to leave the UMC and more people to leave the Methodist Church. The UMC will splinter if it takes a stand that allows LGTBQ clergy and same-sex marriage (this may happen even if the worldwide religion, or the rest of the worldwide religion, keeps the policy). Thus, a splintering is probable with some churches in the United States and worldwide allowing LGTBQ clergy and same-sex marriage and some not; the unknowns are how many will pick each position and what name each branch will be given.

Part of the reason for the contention in the UMC, more so than in other religions, is that the UMC is somewhat known for being more middle of the road on issues, particularly in the United States, than some denominations. This battle would not be expected to break out in 2019 in the Baptist Church, at least not the Southern Baptists. Also, policy is set at a national level, leading to more tension and more notice of the policy. In the Presbyterian Church, for instance, policy is set at a more local level, and ministers are usually picked by the church. This allows for more flexibility, even though policy over same-sex marriage was decided by the Presbyterians at a national level.

Part of the reason for the resistance to change within the UMC in the United States is its location. The UMC is strongest in the American South. This is also the most conservative region of the country historically. The American South has often been the least accepting of anything nontraditional or new, and both of these descriptions apply to same-sex marriage. The church in the American South has also been resistant to change. During the civil rights movement, the white churches were often the most resistant to accepting African Americans.

*See also:* Baptist Church, The; Catholic Church, The; Eastern Orthodox Church, The; Mormons; Presbyterians

## Further Reading

Beneke, Chris, and Christopher S. Grenda. (2015). *The Lively Experiment: Religious Toleration in America from Roger Williams to the Present.* Lanham, MD: Rowman & Littlefield.

Davis, Morris L. (2008). *The Methodist Unification: Christianity and the Politics of Race in the Jim Crow Era.* Religion, Race, and Ethnicity. New York: NYU Press.

Feldman, Glenn. (2005). *Politics and Religion in the White South.* Religion in the South. Lexington: University Press of Kentucky.

Gjelten, Tom. (2019). "After Disagreements over LGBTQ Clergy, U.S. Methodists Move Closer to Split." NPR, "All Things Considered," June 26, 2019. https://

www.npr.org/2019/06/26/736344079/u-s-methodists-meet-to-consider-what
-comes-next-after-disagreements-over-lgbt-cl.

Hastings, Adrian, Alistair Mason, and Hugh S. Pyper. (2000). *The Oxford Companion to Christian Thought*. New York: Oxford University Press.

Oliveto, Karen P. (2018). *Our Strangely Warmed Hearts: Coming Out into God's Call*. Nashville, TN: Abingdon Press.

Waldrep, Christopher. (2012). "The Use and Abuse of the Law: Public Opinion and United Methodist Church Trials of Ministers Performing Same-Sex Union Ceremonies." *Law and History Review* 30 (4): 953–1005.

# Mormons

The Mormon faith is formally known as the Church of Jesus Christ of Latter-day Saints (LDS), but it will be referred to as Mormon here. It is one of the few uniquely American faiths, in that it started in the United States. Joseph Smith, according to the faith, discovered golden plates that told of a new gospel, which became the Book of Mormon. The faith was driven out of several eastern and Midwestern states, including New York. In Illinois, Smith was murdered, and many of his followers subsequently moved to what became Utah. There they engaged in a lengthy battle over marriage—not same-sex marriage, but polygamy, as many of the early leaders, including Smith, had been polygamous. However, the U.S. Supreme Court ruled against the religion, and the religion changed its doctrine. This all occurred before 1900.

In the late 20th century, Mormons moved from political outsiders to insiders and gained considerable power in Utah and elsewhere. They also became a large conservative and business force. Among the prominent Mormon political figures is Mitt Romney, the 2012 Republican presidential candidate and now senator from, not surprisingly, Utah (even though he was previously the governor of Massachusetts).

The Mormon religion has taken a strong stand against same-sex attraction. (In many ways, the Mormon faith has been very conservative in a traditional sense, as it has opposed most changes, including not allowing African Americans into full membership of the church at the lay level before the 1970s.) In terms of same-sex attraction, Mormons had, for a long time, a two-pronged approach against it. They held that sexuality was only appropriate in marriage, and marriage, of course, was only allowed between a man and a woman. This was their stance, and they took strong measures to enforce it. One could basically be banned from full church membership if one was found to be gay or lesbian, even while in an opposite-sex marriage. With the level of power that Mormons held in many areas of Utah, this was the equivalent of being shunned from public life.

The Mormon Church continued these beliefs into the 21st century, with a few notable changes. Up through the 1970s, the church taught that same-sex attraction was "curable," and with enough effort, one could stop being gay or lesbian. The Mormon Church has since ceased that idea. However, even though the church admits that same-sex attraction is not a choice, it still does not allow any form of same-sex sexual expression. In the 2000s, the Mormon Church also worked strongly in California to pass Proposition 8, which amended the California Constitution to ban same-sex marriage; most of the door-to-door volunteers were Mormons. In an interesting development, the Mormon Church supported a proposal in Salt Lake City (where the international Mormon Church is headquartered) to ban discrimination against gay people in some areas even while allowing religious institutions to discriminate. This does show some level of change that has occurred.

The position of the Mormon Church is also changing, due in part perhaps to the reactions of people inside the faith (although the Mormon Church would not indicate that). In 2015, the church had to make a decision on how to deal with the children of same-sex unions, as such unions were now legal across the United States (the church had probably decided before this, but it was announced in late 2015, after *Obergefell*). The church held that the children (as well as those in such unions) were, to use the Mormon term, "apostate," meaning that the person has abandoned their religion or, more practically, could not fully participate in the religion. As the blessing of the church is needed for many Mormon ceremonies, including several that make sure the person is to be fully blessed in the afterlife, this is very important. A sizable number of people left the Mormon Church after this.

In 2019, the Mormon Church reversed itself. It held that there had been another "divine revelation," which meant the church would now allow the children of same-sex unions to be full members of the church in terms of what they received, including baptism. Same-sex unions and same-sex behavior were now held to be merely immoral rather than rising to the level of fully making the person and their family apostate. The announcement made it clear, though, that the people in the same-sex union were still regarded as not being good Mormons.

What level of pressure public opinion played is not known, but it is clear that the Mormon Church wanted the issue solved. The church obviously also wanted to stop losing members. To reverse policy in less than 4 years and without a public vote is unheard of in a large denomination, especially one as controlled by tradition as the Mormon Church. To make a comparison to history, it took nearly 70 years to reverse the polygamy decision, and about 30 of those were spent fighting the U.S. government tooth and nail. So change is occurring more rapidly now than in the past.

*See also:* Baptist Church, The; Catholic Church, The; Eastern Orthodox Church, The; Methodists; Presbyterians

## Further Reading

Bowman, Matthew Burton. (2012). *The Mormon People: The Making of an American Faith*. New York: Random House.
Givens, Terryl, and Reid Larkin Neilson. (2014). *The Columbia Sourcebook of Mormons in the United States*. New York: Columbia University Press.
Gordon, Sarah Barringer. (2002). *The Mormon Question: Polygamy and Constitutional Conflict in Nineteenth-Century America*. Studies in Legal History. Chapel Hill: University of North Carolina Press.
Siker, Jeffrey S., ed. (2007). *Homosexuality and Religion: An Encyclopedia*. Santa Barbara, CA: Greenwood Press.
Stein, Mark. (2014). *American Panic: A History of Who Scares Us and Why*. New York: Palgrave Macmillan.

# N

## New Bills Opposing Same-Sex Marriage

The legal situation of same-sex marriage is settled, but that does not mean that those opposed to marriage equality have been silenced. Opposition to same-sex marriage continues in a number of ways. Whether this opposition will be successful remains to be seen.

In this entry, the opposition will be briefly surveyed before the newer bills are also examined. One way opposition continues is in attempts to nullify the U.S. Supreme Court decision of *Obergefell*. Some have argued in public policy forums that the Supreme Court is not the law of the land. While the Supreme Court does speak for all Americans, this opposition is nothing new. Attempts have been made throughout history to nullify Supreme Court decisions. Perhaps the most well known of these efforts is the Southern opposition to the *Brown v. Board of Education* decision.

Other efforts include allowing opposition under other guises and making efforts to limit the effect of *Obergefell*. Such efforts include bills that allow judges and other legal officials the power to decide who can marry (one can get a license to marry at the courthouse, but no judge has to officiate). This weakens *Obergefell*, as one then has to find another person to officiate at the wedding. Other efforts include removing the idea of the marriage license. Some states have no longer have marriage licenses and simply allow couples to file a marriage contract rather than a marriage license. Those opposed to marriage equality apparently find a marriage contract between two gay people less offensive than a marriage license between those same two people.

One public way that marriage equality is still being opposed is by the passage of new bills and legislative acts. Now, most of these acts do not directly ban same-sex marriage. The reason for this is because most legislatures realize that the Supreme Court is probably not going to directly overturn *Obergefell*. However, the court might allow indirect restrictions. Thus, bills that aim to deny marriage equality while still allowing same-sex marriage have become popular.

Among these bills are some that allow charities to treat those in same-sex marriages differently from those in opposite-sex marriages. Charities often get involved in the administration of adoptions (and sometimes foster care), and so treating same-sex marriages differently (and allowing charities to do so) allows the state and the charity to say that they do not consider those in same-sex marriages to be equal. This is done under the guise of religious freedom.

Another such bill allowed any state employee to deny service when that service affected their religious freedom. Thus, a state employee could deny a marriage license or refuse to file a marriage contract (or any other document). After all, if a state employee is opposed to same-sex marriage, is that state employee required to have any contact with a person in a same-sex marriage? One would think not, and thus, one could get married but then be shunned by society, all in the name of religious freedom.

Some bills do ban same-sex marriage. One that was proposed but not passed would have labeled same-sex marriage a "sham marriage." Another would have labeled opposite-sex marriage a secular institution and then labeled same-sex marriage a religious institution, tying it to a religion of "secular humanism." Then, as the State of Kansas attempted this (which was the state in which all these verbal gymnastics took place), the state would have to ban same-sex marriage, as the state was not allowed to be religious. This perfect 10 in mental contortions never passed.

Religious freedom bills have also popped up in general. Some figures have defended these bills as merely being the same as the federal bill; if the federal Religious Freedom Restoration Act (RFRA) is allowed, these bills should be allowed as well. Of course, as some of the opponents of these state RFRAs have pointed out, if the bills are the same, why is the state bill needed at all.

It should be noted that these bills being discussed are not the only bills that oppose human equality. Many who oppose marriage equality also oppose treating people who are LGBTQ equally. Some bills advanced by this faction include the so-called bathroom bill, which would force transgender people to use the bathroom of their assigned sex at birth rather than the one they identify with. Others include straightforward attempts to shame people who are different, and sometimes these bills are lumped with one that opposes same-sex marriage.

Thus, even while same-sex marriage is the law of the land, this does not mean that all people have fully accepted it. It also does not mean that people have stopped opposing it in the legislatures and the court of public opinion, even while one cannot oppose it in the judicial courts. It also reminds everyone to pay attention to the various backdoors used to achieve one's end, even though the courts have said that the end cannot be achieved.

**See also:** *Masterpiece Cakeshop v. Colorado Civil Rights Commission*; *Obergefell v. Hodges*; Religious Law and Practice in the United States Historically; 2004 Elections and Religion; 2000s, The

## Further Reading

Brandon, Mark E. (2014). "Secession and Nullification in the Twenty-First Century." *Arkansas Law Review (1968–Present)* 67 (1): 91.

Bunch, Kenyon. (2005). "If Racial Desegregation, Then Same-Sex Marriage? Originalism and the Supreme Court's Fourteenth Amendment." *Harvard Journal of Law & Public Policy* 28 (3): 781.

"Legal Recognition of Same-Sex Relationships." (2013). *Georgetown Journal of Gender & the Law* 14 (2): 517–551.

Schwartz, David S. (2019). "McCulloch at 200." *Arkansas Law Review (1968–Present)* 72 (1): 1–5.

Thro, William E. (2011). "The Heart of the Constitutional Enterprise: Affirming Equality and Freedom in Public Education." *Brigham Young University Education & Law Journal* 2011 (2): 571–591.

O

## Obergefell v. Hodges

The *Obergefell* decision meant the end, at least in the courts and legislatures, of the same-sex marriage debate. How people felt in their hearts and minds, and how they would treat those in same-sex marriages, remained to be determined.

In 1996, Congress passed the Defense of Marriage Act (DOMA), which held marriage to be between one man and one woman. Few would have predicted that less than 20 years later the U.S. Supreme Court would strike down that definition and that the nation would react with relative calm, at least among those who favored DOMA's definition.

After DOMA, those favoring marriage equality turned to state courts and state constitutions, as their route in federal courts was barred. They had some success as states started offering other arrangements, such as civil unions, rather than marriage. This debate also caused the average citizen to think about marriage equality. However, this produced little change federally; if a state did not have a civil union, it did not have to even consider recognizing a civil union from elsewhere.

No state had marriage for same-sex couples before 2004. Massachusetts was the first state, and people flocked there to get married. Massachusetts also rejected the "responsible procreation" defense, which held that state recognition of marriage aimed to reward procreation and so was limited to opposite-sex marriage. One article noted that "the Supreme Court of Massachusetts issued its much-anticipated and groundbreaking 4–3 decision in *Goodridge v. Department of Public Health*, which directly rejected the responsible-procreation defense and held that the ban [on same-sex marriage] violated the state constitution" (Nice 2012, 813–814). This started a series of lawsuits as well, to see whether people had a federal right to have their marriage from one state recognized in another.

Churches also had to consider whether to marry same-sex couples. Some churches ruled against it at a denominational level, and some allowed local churches control over the issue. In some cases, local churches defied church policy, leading to schisms. In others, the local clergy favored a policy opposed by his or her congregation. All the controversy led to lots of consideration. The religious debates also helped to shift public opinion. In 1996, very few people favored the rights of gay people to marry. By 2004, it had grown to about 40 percent favoring it. By around 2010, many polls found a near 50–50 split. Those announcing themselves as religious still tended to oppose same-sex marriage, but at the same time, the stance of some churches was driving people away. There was always the question, though, of whether people were answering accurately. One survey noted, "Respondents may lie to pollsters when they believe their true opinion runs counter to perceived societal norms" (Lax, Phillips, and Stollwerk 2016, 511).

With few states having same-sex marriage and no state being forced to recognize another state's same-sex marriage, it was an issue for the states in 2010. Gay and lesbian couples were winning some level of recognition but not full success in most places. Religions were also being forced to deal with the issue. A legal sea change started in 2013 with *Hollingsworth v. Perry* and *United States v. Windsor*. The first dealt with California and the second with DOMA.

In 2008, the California legislature legalized same-sex marriage, but California voters had reversed that with a ballot Proposition 8. Thus, the most populous U.S. state (and one of the most liberal) had voted against same-sex marriage. By 2010, though, California's governor was not defending Proposition 8. A group intervened to defend it, and Proposition 8 was struck down. That case, *Perry*, came to the U.S. Supreme Court at the same time as *Windsor*.

*Windsor* dealt with the part of DOMA requiring the federal government to not recognize same-sex marriage. In the *Windsor* case, DOMA was struck down as it pertained to the federal government because DOMA violated an individual's rights. The court held that when a state allowed people to be married, the federal government was not allowed to discriminate against that group by not recognizing the marriage for federal law. The opinion did not, though, directly take a stand on whether same-sex marriage should be legal. In *Perry*, the group was not allowed to defend Proposition 8, and so California now allowed marriage equality.

Many states took all this as a cue and passed marriage equality. There were only 5 states that legalized same-sex marriage in 2010, but by 2015, it was up to 36. Many religious groups also continued to reconsider their stances.

It was at this stage that *Obergefell v. Hodges* made it all the way to the U.S. Supreme Court. Four circuit courts of appeal had ruled in favor of forcing recognition of same-sex marriage while another had not, which required the Supreme Court to weigh in. In a 5–4 decision, the Supreme Court held that the bans on recognizing same-sex marriage violated both the due process clause and the equal protection clause of the Fourteenth Amendment. One dissent, by Chief Justice Roberts, did note that religious liberty might be put at danger, in his mind, by the majority's decision.

*See also:* Defense of Marriage Act, The; Religious Freedom Restoration Act; 2004 Elections and Religion; 2000s, The; *United States v. Windsor*

## Further Reading

Cain, Patrick N., and David Ramsey, eds. (2017). *American Constitutionalism, Marriage and the Family:* Obergefell v. Hodges *and* U.S. v. Windsor *in Context*. Lanham, MD: Lexington Books.

Dent, George W., Jr. (2017). "Meaningless Marriage: The Incoherent Legacy of *Obergefell v. Hodges.*" *Appalachian Journal of Law* 17: 1–58.

Frank, Nathaniel. (2017). *Awakening: How Gays and Lesbians Brought Marriage Equality to America*. Cambridge, MA: Belknap Press.

Klarman, Michael J. (2013). *From the Closet to the Altar: Courts, Backlash, and the Struggle for Same-Sex Marriage*. Oxford, UK: Oxford University Press.

Lax, Jeffrey R., Justin H. Phillips, and Alissa F. Stollwerk. (2016). "Are Survey Respondents Lying about Their Support for Same-Sex Marriage?" *Public Opinion Quarterly* 80 (2): 510–533.

Nice, Julie A. (2012). "The Descent of Responsible Procreation: A Genealogy of an Ideology." *Loyola of Los Angeles Law Review* 45 (3): 781–847.

Witosky, Tom, and Marc Hansen. (2015). *Equal before the Law: How Iowa Led Americans to Marriage Equality*. Iowa City: University of Iowa Press.

# P

## Pastors vs. Their Churches

Over the past several decades, a large number of pastors (in this entry, "pastors" include imams, rabbis, ministers, and all other clergy) have split from their churches (and mosques, synagogues, and other places of worship) over the issue of same-sex marriage. Some pastors have split over particular marriages, while others have split due to a generally different view. This overall point shows that it is not as simple as some churches believe in same-sex marriage and some oppose, but some ministers differ from their own congregations or denominations. The end result is varied as well. Some pastors rejoined their initial churches after a time, some led their own congregations away from the religion, and others formed their own churches.

One pastor who split from his church was Frank Schaefer. He performed a same-sex marriage in the United Methodist Church, which was in violation of the Methodist regulations at the time. He did, though, have a bit of personal motivation to perform the marriage, as it was his son who was getting married. In 2013, he performed the marriage in violation of church policy, and by the end of the year, he had been removed from the Methodist Church. Since his removal, he has moved churches, and his defrocking (the official term for being stripped from the Methodist Church) was overturned. He is now working in California. This shows that same-sex marriage can cause some pastors to be forced to choose between their church and their beliefs, and sometimes the beliefs win. Of course, sometimes the church wins, but that would be more difficult to prove.

Some pastors have also led their local congregation in rebellions against their overall church. This is a different sense of how pastors have revolted against their churches. One such example of a rebellion is the Reverend Dr. Nancy Petty, who leads the Pullen Memorial Baptist Church in North Carolina. Petty was one of the first to welcome the LGBTQ community. In response, the church was removed from the Southern Baptist Convention. However, her church has continued to back her. She now leads the Pullen church as an independent Baptist church.

The people who have set out to form their own religions over the issue are a third example of rebellion. They are more difficult to document, unless they also formed a religious structure at the same time. While she did not form her own religion, Mahdia Lynn founded a mosque in Chicago that aimed to be LGBTQ friendly. Others created their own brand of Christianity to welcome all. Elijah Walker is a transgender pastor, and he founded Solomon's Porch in Jonesboro Arkansas, a small city in northern Arkansas. He realized that he needed to found an organization that was welcoming to all. While this might be expected in Chicago, it would probably not be expected in a small city in rural Arkansas, and it shows that this issue is present all across the country.

All of this fits into the same-sex marriage and religion discussion, as it shows that while the largest religions are often discussed, one size does not fit all. Many people's answer to a religion that does not fit their needs is to leave it, and a pastor who leaves a religion either has to find a new one, start his or her own, or find a new job. Thus, it is not surprising that religious figures who want to have marriage equality but are in a religion that does not welcome same-sex marriage form their own religion (just as some people's answer to a religion that welcomes same-sex marriage is to leave that religion). The examples discussed here also prove the universality of the debate. Muslims, Baptists, and Methodists all had issues of rebellion against what their central religious structures said, even though those central groups might agree on little else.

*See also:* Islam; Methodists; New Bills Opposing Same-Sex Marriage; *Obergefell v. Hodges*; Religious Groups Splintering

## Further Reading

Associated Press. (2013). "Church Jury Convicts Pastor Who Performed Son's Gay Marriage." *The Spectator* (Hamilton, Ontario).

Cadge, Wendy, Heather Day, and Christopher Wildeman. (2007). "Bridging the Denomination-Congregation Divide: Evangelical Lutheran Church in America Congregations Respond to Homosexuality." *Review of Religious Research* 48 (3): 245.

Gadoua, Renee K. (2013). "Methodist Pastor Faces Penalty over Gay Weddings." *Christian Century* 25: 13.

Karsten, J. L. (2014). "Adam and Adam: Or Eve and Eve?" *JEPTA: Journal of the European Pentecostal Theological Association* 34 (1): 1–14.

London, Emily, Maggie Siddiqi, and Luke Wallis. (2019). "9 LGBTQ Faith Leaders to Watch in 2019." Center for American Progress, September 9, 2019. https://www.americanprogress.org/issues/religion/news/2019/09/09/474156/9 -lgbtq-faith-leaders-watch-2019/.

Stoneburner, Beth. (2019). "A Transgender Pastor Begins an LGBTQ-Inclusive Church in Arkansas." Friendly Atheist, June 11, 2019. https://friendlyatheist .patheos.com/2019/06/11/a-transgender-pastor-began-an-lgbtq-inclusive -church-in-arkansas/.

Waldrep, Christopher. (2012). "The Use and Abuse of the Law: Public Opinion and United Methodist Church Trials of Ministers Performing Same-Sex Union Ceremonies." *Law and History Review* 30 (4): 953.

# Pavan v. Smith

The *Pavan* case arose out of Arkansas and the question of who is listed on birth certificates. Two different lesbian married couples filed lawsuits after giving birth in the state. Both couples were married outside of the state and had moved into it. The law in question dealt with a provision that required the father of the child to be listed, even if he was not the biological father of the child, and forbid the listing of both lesbians on the birth certificate. The court, in a per curiam opinion (one that is collectively signed by all the justices who agree with it) said that the law discriminated. Three justices dissented. They argued that the law was only being challenged when dealing with children who were born through artificial insemination and so should not have been struck down as a whole.

The law did deal with issues of opposite-sex couples who had children through artificial insemination. The man married to the woman at the time of birth was still listed as the father, even if he was not the biological father (i.e., his sperm was not used for the artificial insemination). In all cases, the woman who gave birth was treated as the mother (nothing was noted about egg donation). (Also, in both cases involved in this lawsuit, the sperm donation was anonymous, so there was no biological father to even consider listing on the birth certificate.)

The per curiam decision first summarized the facts of the case and lower court rulings. The trial court had held for the two couples, but the Arkansas Supreme Court had viewed the statute as being related to biology, not marriage, and so differentiated it from *Obergefell*. The fact that the biology in question was one of gender (male spouses were listed but female spouses were not), and so stemmed from same-sex marriage, was not a focus of the Arkansas Supreme Court. The Arkansas Supreme Court defended the birth certificate as a way of memorializing a child's parents. However, it was not clear why opposite-sex parents should be able to memorialize the birth but not same-sex parents. The U.S. Supreme Court noted, "But Arkansas law makes birth certificates about more than just genetics" (Majority). Birth certificates have been made by Arkansas, the court noted, as a way to denote married parentage and so hold value.

Three justices dissented in an opinion written by Justice Gorsuch. Gorsuch's main argument was that the majority went too far. First, the dissenters agreed with the state that "government officials can identify public health trends and helping individuals determine their biological lineage, citizenship, or susceptibility to genetic disorders" (Dissent). However, as the father listed did not have to be the biological father, this reasoning is somewhat suspect. Second, the dissent held that the two couples were not challenging the law specifically, and so the law should not have been reversed. Third, the dissent held that the summary reversal would not add that much more than what had already been done, as the state had admitted (apparently) that other benefits would be available to nonbiological parents, regardless of whether they were in same-sex or opposite-sex marriages. Finally, throughout the dissent, it also attempted to stand on history and commonality. It argued that many other states did it and that it had been done for a long time and so was allowable. Gorsuch's dissent was joined by Justices Thomas and Alito, the other two most conservative justices on the court. This was an argument of opposition to the decision (and continuing a quiet objection to *Obergefell*) while focusing on the breadth of the remedy used.

However, what the dissent misses, and what the per curiam implies but does not state specifically, is that the court appears tired of having states uphold discrimination against married same-sex couples under questionable justification when *Obergefell* seemed to have settled the manner. Perhaps the dissent did not miss this, though, and wanted to suggest that this tired attitude was not the correct one. It may have also been a sign to those opposed to same-sex marriage to keep fighting it on the margins, as only two more votes would be needed to limit same-sex marriage rights in some ways. It should be noted that religion was never used as a justification, and Arkansas appears to have offered little justification other than possible genetic disorders and an argument that the law did not discriminate.

*Pavan* proves that, like many issues, the landmark case did not end the issue. For example, in education, *Brown v. Board of Education* by no means ended the issue of segregated schools, and *Obergefell* did not end discrimination against same-sex couples who wanted to marry. Many laws, regardless of their official or actual purpose, discriminated against same-sex couples. State courts, for a variety of reasons, do not see the laws as discriminatory. Thus, the U.S. Supreme Court must act to end that discrimination. However, not all of the Supreme Court is fully on board. What the future holds for the issue is anyone's guess.

**See also:** Adoption; *Obergefell v. Hodges*; Religious Freedom Restoration Act; State Laws on Religious Freedom; Surrogacy

## Further Reading

Ball, Carlos A. (2016). *After Marriage Equality: The Future of LGBT Rights*. New York: New York University Press.

Brennan, Jason. (2012). *Libertarianism: What Everyone Needs to Know*. What Everyone Needs to Know. New York: Oxford University Press.

Cleves, Rachel Hope. (2014). *Charity and Sylvia: A Same-Sex Marriage in Early America*. New York: Oxford University Press.

Dissent. *Pavan* v. *Smith*. https://supreme.justia.com/cases/federal/us/582/16-992 /#tab-opinion-3752821.

Majority. *Pavan* v. *Smith*. https://supreme.justia.com/cases/federal/us/582/16-992 /#tab-opinion-3752820.

Nugent, Walter T. K. (2010). *Progressivism: A Very Short Introduction*. Very Short Introductions. New York: Oxford University Press.

Stein, Mark. (2014). *American Panic: A History of Who Scares Us and Why*. London: Palgrave Macmillan.

Tobias, Sarah. (2010). *Policy Issues Affecting Lesbian, Gay, Bisexual, and Transgender Families*. Ann Arbor: University of Michigan Press.

# Pentecostals

The Pentecostal area of religion spans a wide variety of churches. These include the Church of God, the Church of God in Christ, and the Pentecostal Holiness Church, among others. Pentecostals in general believe that one must have a direct connection with the Holy Spirit. These include, for many, things like speaking in tongues, and most faiths that are Pentecostal have a belief in divine healing. Most of these faiths oppose same-sex marriage and tend to oppose same-sex attraction in general.

The Church of God discussed in this entry is the Church of God whose national headquarters is in Cleveland, Tennessee. While it describes itself as the Church of God (and has staked a claim to that name), it titles itself Church of God (Cleveland, Tennessee) to clarify which one it is. It is the largest group of this name with a claim of over seven million U.S. members. (It should be noted that the Church of God in Christ, with that slightly different name, is sometimes ranked as larger.)

The Church of God calls for a requirement of "moral purity." Thus, all sin is banned (which is not that much different from other churches), but it also requires a move away from lust. One element of this is a ban on same-sex attraction. In conjunction with this, it is not surprising that same-sex marriages are not allowed in the church, and gay people are not allowed to be pastors. Baptisms of the children of same-sex couples are also generally not allowed. This mirrors the larger Pentecostal movement of which the Church of God is a part.

The Church of God in Christ discussed in this entry is headquartered in Memphis, Tennessee. This church is predominately African American and has over six million members. It started around the beginning of the 20th century, being incorporated in 1907. It is a Pentecostal church and, similar to many other Pentecostal movements, considers same-sex attraction to be a sin. Consequently, same-sex marriages are not allowed. The Church of God in Christ was very active, though, in fighting for the civil rights of African Americans. In many ways, the Church of God in Christ is a result of the activities of one man, H. C. Mason, who founded it and led it for 64 years.

A third group is the Pentecostal Holiness Church, which is headquartered in Oklahoma City under the auspices of the International Pentecostal Holiness Church. It is largely in the Southeast of the United States, but several of its well-known figures, such as Oral Roberts, were more in the area of Oklahoma. The Pentecostal Holiness Church condemns any changes in recent "sexual morality," holding that everything declined starting in the 1960s. All same-sex behavior is viewed as immoral, and so same-sex marriages are also banned.

Most Pentecostal denominations, if not all, believe that the Bible is both infallible and literally true. Thus, most of the language in the Bible that could be taken to ban same-sex attraction is not interpreted but merely read, which in turn leads to bans on same-sex behavior. Pentecostals also have a variety of other beliefs that set them apart from other Protestants (generally), such as a belief in faith healing and the ability to speak in tongues, but these beliefs generally do not seem to have affected their feelings toward gay people. For nearly all Pentecostal denominations, it would seem, the ban on same-sex marriages in the church extends to not baptizing the children of same-sex marriages. (It is unknown, of course, how many same-sex couples attend these churches, but the number is probably small.)

Most research on the Pentecostals has looked at the Pentecostals outside the United States. The reaction of the Pentecostal bodies in other countries has been muted to same-sex marriage. About the Netherlands, one author wrote, "There were no petitions by Pentecostal churches to stop the same-sex law being passed, nor can I find official denominational declarations against it. Even critical articles appear to be absent. The law was presumably ignored. To date I know of no same-sex marriage being church blessed in a Pentecostal church. I am aware of a same-sex male couple who attend a Pentecostal church" (Karsten 2014, 13).

In England, Pentecostal protests (and general lack of awareness in the country) did not combine to slow down the process. One author noted that there was little discussion and so little protest of same-sex marriage.

What was surprising to many voters was that this was not a matter that was ever discussed before the general election when Cameron gained power. There were no television debates upon the subject, no radio phone-in programs, no discussions in newspapers about same-sex marriage and no grassroots campaigning. Indeed, when Cameron began to advocate same-sex marriage, the LGBTQ community appeared to be taken by surprise. Civil partnerships appeared to have put straight and gay communities on an equal footing. The government launched what it called "a consultation" although those who filled in the online survey could see the government's mind was made up; it intended to push through a policy that was only open to minor modification. Despite opposition in both Houses of Parliament and a huge petition carrying over half a million signatures, the government passed the same-sex marriage law marriage bill into law in 2013. (Kay 2014, 21)

*See also:* Baptist Church, The; History and Religion; Mennonites; Methodists; 2000s, The

## Further Reading

Crew, Michael. (1990). *The Church of God: A Social History*. Knoxville: University of Tennessee Press.

Jacobsen, Douglas. (2003). *Thinking in the Spirit: Theologies of the Early Pentecostal Movement*. Bloomington: Indiana University Press.

Karsten, J. L. (2014). "Adam and Adam: Or Eve and Eve?" *JEPTA: Journal of the European Pentecostal Theological Association* 34 (1): 1–14.

Kay, William K. (2014). "Year of the Family: Recent Changes to Marriage Law in the UK." *JEPTA: Journal of the European Pentecostal Theological Association* 34 (1): 19–24.

Robins, R. G. (2004). *A.J. Tomlinson: Plainfolk Modernist*. Religion in America. New York: Oxford University Press.

Synan, Vinson. (1997). *The Holiness-Pentecostal Tradition: Charismatic Movements in the Twentieth Century*. Grand Rapids, MI: William B. Eerdmans.

Wacker, Grant. (2001). *Heaven Below: Early Pentecostals and American Culture*. Cambridge, MA: Harvard University Press.

# Presbyterians

The Presbyterian Church in the United States has a couple of different major branches. The main one considered in this entry is the Presbyterian Church (USA), known by the abbreviation PC(USA), which is a 1983 merger of the Presbyterian Church in the United States and the United Presbyterian Church in the United States of America. The PC(USA) now has about 1.3 million members. In the 19th century, the Presbyterians, like other denominations, had split over slavery into northern and southern factions.

The Presbyterian Church differs from other churches in several ways, but one of the largest is in the area of control; each church has a fair amount of power, and each pastor does as well. The pastor is picked by the local church rather than being assigned. The PC(USA) is more welcoming of diversity than some of the other Presbyterian branches, but Presbyterians are still more monocultural than the United States as a whole.

As of the early 21st century, the Presbyterian Church was no stranger to the LGBTQ issue. In the 1980s, a movement called the More Light Churches Network worked within and around the PC(USA) to welcome all people. The PC(USA) slowly responded, moving first to adopt a regulation in 1996 that required either chastity or sex within an opposite-sex marriage. This covered all ordained church officials, including those who were from the congregations, which is very important in the Presbyterian Church, as a lot of power rests at the local level. By 2011, the regulation was removed, allowing for LGBTQ ministers as well as elected officials.

The PC(USA) was fully embroiled in the same-sex marriage controversy. A fair number of congregations left the PC(USA) when it allowed local congregations to choose, and some of those who left aligned with more conservative umbrella groups, such as the Association of Confessing Evangelicals. Others moved to different branches of the Presbyterian Church.

In 2014, the PC(USA) General Assembly voted to allow same-sex marriages but did not compel clergy to perform them. This moved the battle down to the local level but also drove some churches out of the PC(USA) to other groups once again. It should be noted that the presbytery, at the local level, owns the church property, not the church, and so if a church chooses to leave the denomination, the presbytery owns the property. Of course, some churches in the PC(USA) have been more welcoming to LGBTQ people (and elders, deacons and ministers, once allowed) than others throughout.

Another branch of the Presbyterian Church is the Presbyterian Church of America (PCA). It has around 400,000 members and is the second-largest denomination. The PCA is bigger in some parts of the United States than the PC(USA), including some regions of the American South, and is more conservative than the PC(USA). The formal church formed in 1973.

The ordination of women was one of the early ideas that marked the split, with the churches that were in the PCA not willing to accept what became the PC(USA)'s stance that women could be ordained (the PCA's position was that no woman in any Presbyterian church could be a minister, while the PC(USA) allowed women to be ordained and then allowed the local church to decide could be their minister).

Opposition to civil rights also played a role in the split, with the PCA churches being more opposed to civil rights (the PCA has since officially apologized). The PCA churches also oppose change, and so it should be no surprise that these churches oppose the inclusion of LGBTQ people. They also, obviously, oppose same-sex marriage.

The Cumberland Presbyterian Church formed in the early 19th century in the Cumberland River valley. The denomination was generally more conservative than other early Presbyterian groups, but in the early 1900s, the denomination split in half, with many joining the Presbyterian

Church in the United States (a forerunner, as noted, of PC(USA)). The remaining churches are generally cordial with PC(USA) but oppose PC(USA)'s stance toward same-sex attraction. They also oppose same-sex marriage.

These two branches, the PCA and the Cumberland Presbyterian Church, are the next two largest after the PC(USA). Between the two branches, they have about 2,600 congregations, but they are by no means the only other branches. There are also probably nearly that many other Presbyterian churches out there, and they probably represent at least a dozen or more other branches of the Presbyterian Church.

*See also:* Baptist Church, The; Catholic Church, The; Methodists; Pentecostals; 2000s, The

## Further Reading

Burgess, John P. (1999). "Framing the Homosexuality Debate Theologically: Lessons from the Presbyterian Church (U.S.A.)." *Review of Religious Research* 41 (2): 262–274. https://doi.org/10.2307/3512110.

Butler, Jon, Randall Herbert Balmer, and Grant Wacker. (2008). *Religion in American Life: A Short History*. Updated ed. New York: Oxford University Press.

Clarke, Erskine. (1996). *Our Southern Zion: A History of Calvinism in the South Carolina Low Country, 1690–1990*. Tuscaloosa: University of Alabama Press.

Hastings, Adrian, Alistair Mason, and Hugh S. Pyper. (2000). *The Oxford Companion to Christian Thought*. New York: Oxford University Press.

Lantzer, Jason S. (2012). *Mainline Christianity: The Past and Future of America's Majority Faith*. New York: NYU Press.

# R

## Religion and Interracial Marriage

While this book is largely about same-sex marriage and religion, many of the same arguments used against same-sex marriage were also used against interracial marriage. In addition, many churches reacted in similar ways to those involved in interracial marriages (and the practice) as they reacted to same-sex marriages in the 1990s and 2000s.

One might think that the issue of interracial marriage is long in the past. After all, it was 1967 when the U.S. Supreme Court outlawed a ban on interracial marriage. However, churches (and church-affiliated organizations) were slow to react. One of the highest profile such institutions was Liberty Baptist University (now just Liberty). Liberty Baptist seemed to have banned interracial dating, which is obviously a step past banning interracial marriage.

Another college that banned interracial dating was Bob Jones University in the 1970s. This became well known in the 1980s when the IRS removed the tax exemption for Bob Jones, and the university took the case all the way to the U.S. Supreme Court. At the Supreme Court, the university defended the practice as being allowed under religious liberty. The Supreme Court did not agree and ruled for the IRS in an 8–1 decision. The only justice who favored Bob Jones was William Rehnquist, a future chief justice. As late as 1998, the university defended its ideas, holding that "God has separated people for his own purposes. He has erected barriers between the nations, not only land and sea barriers, but also ethnic, cultural, and language barriers. God has made people different from one another and intends those differences to remain. Bob Jones University is opposed to intermarriage of the races because it breaks down the barriers God has established" (http://www.jbhe.com/news_views/62_bobjones.html). That sounds very similar to the language in the district court opinion in *Loving* over 30 years earlier. The university formally reversed its stance three years later.

Some churches have also formally opposed interracial couples. These include the Gulnare Free Will Baptist Church in Kentucky. The church held that spouses in interracial marriages were not allowed (presumably the person in question had married someone who was already a member or the idea applied to both). All were held welcome to attend, but not everyone could fully participate. This was claimed to promote unity, which is an interesting religious goal, and the policy did not take a stand on whether those in interracial marriages were saved. This is definitely an interesting use of religious liberty, and the preacher of the church actually opposed the church's decision. This was a very small congregation, as the vote was 9 to 6 to ban the couple in question. The preacher soon afterward overturned the vote as being procedurally improper.

These examples are obviously only churches that took formal votes against interracial marriage. Many other times, churches informally counseled spouses against marrying or a church may not have welcomed a spouse fully into the church, even when the other half of the marrying couple had previously been welcome. There are many steps to full membership, and the formal vote is well down that list of steps in terms of how often it is used to limit a member.

For some groups, religion increases opposition to interracial marriage. According to Perry, "For white Americans, religious heritage has a clear ethno-racial component. That is to say, the more whites desire their descendants to share the same religious creeds, values, and rituals, the more they would prefer that these descendants be themselves white, and thus, religious heritage is to a large degree equated with whiteness" (Perry 2014, 203). This in turn is obviously tied to an opposition to interracial marriage. These same ideas may also be tied to an opposition to same-sex marriage, as these groups want their children to look like them, and none of them, obviously, had same-sex marriages. There were LGBTQ individuals in the past, but those people painting the picture of the United States looking like them would not have admitted it.

This opposition to intermarriage may also be tied in with a desire to make the United States into a Christian nation, or what is called *Christian nationalism*. Perry and Whitehead wrote, "The results from this research extend our understanding of the intersections of social identities, persistent racial exclusion and contemporary national politics by highlighting a potential mechanism linking revitalized efforts to 'preserve' or 'recover'

America's 'Christian heritage' on the Religious Right with covertly racist intent, and ultimately contributing to the fortification of racial boundaries" (Perry and Whitehead 2015, 1672). This creation of a "Christian heritage" nation is ultimately a white one, with all white families; there is no room for interracial families. There is also no room for same-sex marriages, and so religion (or some types of it) may play a role in encouraging opposition to interracial and same-sex marriages.

*See also:* Baptist Church, The; Chalcedon Movement; Generational Differences; *Loving v. Virginia*; Religious Law and Practice in the United States Historically

## Further Reading

"Bob Jones University Apologizes for Its Racist Past." *Journal of Blacks in Higher Education.* https://www.jbhe.com/news_views/62_bobjones.html.

Botham, Fay. (2009). *Almighty God Created the Races: Christianity, Interracial Marriage, & American Law.* Chapel Hill: University of North Carolina Press.

Davies, Sharon L. (2010). *Rising Road: A True Tale of Love, Race, and Religion in America.* New York: Oxford University Press.

Noble Maillard, Kevin, and Rose Cuison Villazor. (2012). Loving v. Virginia *in a Post-Racial World: Rethinking Race, Sex, and Marriage.* Cambridge, UK: Cambridge University Press.

O'Toole, James M. (2002). *Passing for White: Race, Religion, and the Healy Family, 1820–1920.* Amherst: University of Massachusetts Press.

Perry, Samuel L. (2014). "Hoping for a Godly (White) Family: How Desire for Religious Heritage Affects Whites' Attitudes toward Interracial Marriage." *Journal for the Scientific Study of Religion* 53 (1): 202–218.

Perry, Samuel L., and Andrew L. Whitehead. (2015). "Christian Nationalism and White Racial Boundaries: Examining Whites' Opposition to Interracial Marriage." *Ethnic & Racial Studies* 38 (10): 1671–1689.

Yancey, George A., and Richard Lewis Jr. (2009). *Interracial Families: Current Concepts and Controversies.* Abingdon, UK: Routledge.

## Religious Freedom Restoration Act

The Religious Freedom Restoration Act (RFRA) claimed to restore religious freedom by forcing the federal and state governments to justify any restriction of religious freedom. It was enacted in 1993. The act has had a tortured existence. Its creation and use have been much more involved in politics than in religious freedom or its restoration. The picture one gets of those whose religious freedom is being violated is of a downtrodden minority with no resources and few allies. That, in some ways, was how the case started. It has not been, however, how the act has been utilized since its passage.

This case started in something rare in politics, in most people's eyes, and something nonreligious. The rare thing was the telling of a truth, and the nonreligious item was unemployment compensation. Alfred Smith, a Native American and a drug counselor, had participated in a religious ceremony and ingested peyote. When asked about the ceremony, he admitted the use (if he had denied it, the issue would have ended) and was fired. He applied for unemployment compensation and was denied, as the drug use was considered misconduct and being fired for misconduct meant no unemployment compensation. He appealed the case all the way to the U.S. Supreme Court, which focused not on the issue of whether unemployment compensation could be denied for misconduct (the original issue) but whether the state could ban peyote use. The Supreme Court, in an opinion by Justice Scalia, allowed this, holding that the law banning peyote use was a general law, not one targeting religion. Scalia wrote, "We have never held that an individual's religious beliefs excuse him from compliance with an otherwise valid law prohibiting conduct that the State is free to regulate" (*Oregon v. Smith* 1990, 878–879). As nearly all laws that affect religion are written generally, this case produced outrage and a push for a law protecting religious freedom.

The result was the Religious Freedom Restoration Act. This held that all acts passed by the state or federal governments needed to either not substantially burden freedom of religion or to be justified by a compelling government interest, and they needed to be the least restrictive way to achieve that compelling government interest. This was seen as restoring what many thought the rule was before in the *Sherbert* and *Yoder* cases, but other observers have noted that religious restrictions were normally upheld in the years between *Sherbert* and *Smith*. They had just not created the firestorm that the *Smith* decision did.

RFRA was quickly put to the test, and in 1997, it was struck down as it related to the states, as Congress is not allowed to restrict what states can do under the idea of federalism. Congress did, however, pass the Religious Land Use and Institutionalized Persons Act (RLUIPA). This aimed to strengthen RFRA against the states. However, more questions have arisen, particularly in the area of what constitutes a land-use regulation, and religious institutions have had mixed success. In the prisons, which is what "institutionalized persons" refer to, prisoners have been more successful, although confusion remains. "RLUIPA similarly called for strict scrutiny in reviewing policies of state prisons; yet again, courts differed regarding when and how they should defer to such policies" ("Religious Land Use and Institutionalized Persons Act" 2015, 358).

RFRA, however, was upheld as it related to the federal government in 2006 in the *Gonzales* case, where the federal government was prohibited from preventing a church from using a tea that contained mescaline. Mescaline is an otherwise controlled substance, but the federal government could not show a compelling interest in not allowing the Native American Church to have an exception to this policy. "Gonzales gave RFRA such a vigorous interpretation that religious believers seemed almost better off now than before Smith, at least with respect to federal law" (Lund 2010, 466).

RFRA continued to grow after *Gonzales* with the passage of the Affordable Care Act and other regulations. In 1993, only three in Congress had voted against RFRA. However, those who felt that current culture was demeaning religion saw RFRA as a way to thwart government actions that produced change. With the Affordable Care Act, once it was passed and upheld, some turned to RFRA to resist its mandates. Some had originally opposed the Affordable Care Act as socialism (which they saw as diametrically opposed to religion), and so the turn to RFRA was not as radical as it might seem. Others just opposed the Affordable Care Act in general, and when it was upheld by the U.S. Supreme Court, any other legal reason to oppose it would do. Eventually, some corporations opposed the Affordable Care Act, claiming their religious rights were violated. This is what produced the *Hobby Lobby* case, also known as *Burwell v. Hobby Lobby*, which was decided in 2014.

In *Burwell*, the company argued that a requirement in the Affordable Care Act that mandated that certain contraceptives be covered violated its religious freedom and that a corporation should be treated as a person. The Hobby Lobby Corporation won, not because of the restriction on religious liberty but more because the requirement was not done in the least restrictive way possible. Thus, a restriction on religious liberty may still be upheld if the state can prove that the action was taken in the least restrictive way possible. In the *Burwell* case, the government could force the insurance company to pay for the contraceptives as long as the corporation announced that it was not doing so. This decision has less relevance now, as the Trump administration (as of the time of this writing) has decided to allow corporations to not offer that coverage in any form, whether paid for by the corporation or the insurance company.

How much religious freedom a corporation should have and whether RFRA aimed to cover insurance companies are questions that are still open for discussion. Thus, a law written to help a Native American celebrate his religion (or at least not suffer for celebrating it) has been adapted to help a company. This in turn has an implication for same-sex marriage, as those opposed to it argue that being forced to serve these couples violates their religion. RFRA might allow those opposed out of serving if they can prove that there is a less restrictive way to satisfy the same goal or that the goal is not a fundamental objective.

**See also:** *Baehr v. Miike*; Defense of Marriage Act, The; *Obergefell v. Hodges*; *United States v. Windsor*

## Further Reading

Hamilton, Marci. (2005). *God vs. the Gavel: Religion and the Rule of Law*. New York: Cambridge University Press.

Long, Carolyn Nestor. (2000). *Religious Freedom and Indian Rights: The Case of* Oregon v. Smith. Lawrence: University Press of Kansas.

Lund, Christopher C. (2010). "Religious Liberty after Gonzales: A Look at State RFRAS." *South Dakota Law Review* 3: 466.

National Archives. (n.d.). "The National Archives Experience. Constitution of the United States." Amendments 11–27. http://www.archives.gov/national-archives -experience/charters/constitution_amendments_11-27.html.

*Oregon v. Smith*, 494 U.S. 872 (1990).

"Religious Land Use and Institutionalized Persons Act—Religious Liberty—*Holt v. Hobbs*." (2015). *Harvard Law Review* 129 (1): 351–360.

Seelye, James E., Jr., and Steven A. Littleton, eds. (2013). *Voices of the American Indian Experience*. Santa Barbara, CA: Greenwood.

U.S. Code. "Title 42, 2000bb, 2000bb-1: Congressional Findings and Declaration of Purposes [Relating to RFRA]." https://www.law.cornell.edu/uscode/text/42 /2000bb.

# Religious Groups Splintering

Religious groups have splintered throughout the past, but groups have also splintered today over same-sex marriage. Many people think of religious groups as monolithic, but nothing could be further from the truth. Many individual churches, parishes, or synagogues have been greatly shaped by a pastor or a rabbi, but often what differentiates them, over time, from another church, parish, or synagogue of the same religion is religious doctrine. Some of those were chosen in the moment, and sometimes those differences are what created that church.

A couple of historical examples should suffice to prove that divisions are nothing new. When the Christian church was being founded in the late Roman Empire, divisions over icons and power led to the foundings of what became the Roman Catholic Church and the Eastern Orthodox Church. Of course, each group thought that it had the doctrines correct. Later on, when Protestantism was being founded, Lutheranism and the Baptist faiths formed, in part, over what the importance of baptism was and whether one had to be an adult to be baptized. Lest one think that all early faiths survived, in the early years of Protestantism, there were also the Melchiorites, which ended fairly quickly in the mid-16th century.

The United States was no exception to the idea that religious groups might splinter. In the 19th century, all three major American Protestant religions (Baptists, Methodists, and Presbyterians) split over slavery (although there were also a number of other splits as well), and two of these three breaks occurred in the 1840s (1844 and 1845). The Presbyterians were the relative latecomer to the party, splitting in 1861 after the Civil War began. These churches reunited, generally, in the 20th century, although this activity was spread out over a longer time period.

Churches have also been splintering over same-sex marriage. Before same-sex marriage was allowed in many churches, preachers had to decide whether they would follow their conscience and unite two people of the same sex who loved each other or follow church doctrine. Few preachers, though, suffered any ill effects from violating state law if they married such people. Individual churches had to decide whether they would follow their leader or their church doctrine in such a case.

Small subdenominations also broke off. In the case of the Anglican Church, which has had a number of fissures over the years, same-sex marriage (along with the election of a gay bishop) caused the creation of the Fellowship of Confessing Anglicans. It should be noted that the Anglicans generally would have probably been okay with a gay bishop, as long as the person was publicly celibate, but the person in question was married and so was obviously not celibate (nor did he pretend to be so). Other splinter groups followed, and the election of a gay bishop along with same-sex marriage became just part of a larger debate about whether the Anglican Church was staying true to the word of God.

The most recent (or at least the most recent high-profile) division of a church (and this appears to be a general split rather than a splintering, as noted with the Anglicans) is the United Methodist Church (UMC). Unlike some churches, the UMC sets its policy worldwide. So, it is not a question of what American UMC members want to do but what UMC members worldwide want to do. The UMC has been debating same-sex marriage and gay or lesbian bishops for a number of years in their General Conferences (which meet every four years) and finally decided to allow the church to split. This vote was supposed to take place in May 2020, but COVID-19 occurred. Most observers think that the vote will eventually pass. Conversely, few think that if the vote fails in the 2020 General Conference, the issue will go away forever; in other words, the church will eventually split over the issue.

The UMC is unlikely to be the last religious group to splinter, but it is the largest in the United States to split over it (and probably will be for some time). If one examines the other top 10 (other than those listed as "nonspecified") largest U.S. denominations, the Presbyterians (PC(USA)), Anglicans, and Lutherans (ELCA) have already allowed for marriage equality. The Methodists were dealt with here. The Catholic religion and Baptists are unlikely to adopt marriage equality anytime soon, something that can also be said of the Pentecostals and Holiness groups. That leaves only what some of have called the Restorationists, who want the old times to be restored (once again, a group unlikely to adopt marriage equality), and then the Congregationalists, who allow each congregation to decide, and this level of self-government probably limits the chance for a split.

*See also:* Baptist Church, The; Catholic Church, The; Eastern Orthodox Church, The; Methodists; Presbyterians

## Further Reading

Holzer, Shannon. (2015). "Religious Reasoning and Due Process of the Law: Why Religious Citizens Have the Burden to Prove the Innocence of Their Reasoning in the Public Square." *Journal of Church & State* 57 (3): 419–449.

Johnson, Jill M., David L. Barnhart, Rebekah Jordan Gienapp, and Alex Joyner. (2017). *Living Faithfully: Human Sexuality and the United Methodist Church.* Nashville, TN: Abingdon Press.

Waldrep, Christopher. (2012). "The Use and Abuse of the Law: Public Opinion and United Methodist Church Trials of Ministers Performing Same-Sex Union Ceremonies." *Law and History Review* 30 (4): 953.

Wood, John Halsey, Jr. (2005). "The 1861 Spring Resolutions: Charles Hodge, the American Union, and the Dissolution of the Old School Church." *Journal of Church and State* 47 (2): 371.

## Religious Law and Practice in the United States Historically

Religious law has not had a large effect on the United States historically, despite many people's claims to the contrary. When the country was first founded, a variety of legal systems existed. Most states used a combination of Blackstone's ideas and English law. Louisiana was an exception, as it largely used French Law due to the long-term French influence. The Napoleonic Code, which formed part of French law, had no religious content. The English common law recognizes judge-made law, while the Napoleonic Code suggests that there is a written code of law that controls everything. Of course, the English common law allows for more religious influence, as it is made by judges, but it also allows for more change because it is not codified.

Religious law, though, did not generally impact even those areas with English law. Religious law here would not be things like not killing (although some think of it as that). The Code of Hammurabi, in antiquity-banned killing (even though it based its penalty in part on who was killed), and that was more a code of the state than religion. It also was not a code whose authority was based in any religion that was in the United States at its founding. Thus, while Christian religious law said not to kill, the bans on murder in the early United States did not come from Christian religious law, as nearly all religions banned killing.

Christian laws had more impact in society, as many things were banned on one's religious day. For instance, in many societies, one was not allowed to buy alcohol in general or to buy it on a holy day. These so-called blue laws existed into the 20th century. This matters in the area of same-sex marriage, as some argue (and more argued before *Obergefell*) that since religious law impacted the United States, the religious bans on same-sex activity should be allowed to prevent marriage equality.

Religious law also stayed out of U.S. law in the area of divorce. In much of Europe, the church had to approve divorces (remember Henry VIII's desire for a divorce that led to the creation of the Church of England), but in the United States, divorces never had to be approved by a religious court. Again, this argues against any religion's ban on same-sex marriage being allowed to enter state law for that reason alone.

There were, however, some religious overtones in the state constitutions that existed until the 20th century. For instance, Maryland had a "test oath" in its constitution. That test oath held that one was required to be a Christian to be an officeholder. Maryland's oath stated, "That no other test or qualification ought to be required . . . than such oath of support and fidelity to this State . . . and a declaration of a belief in the Christian religion." Thus, one had to be a Christian, but there was no discrimination between the branches of Christianity. How rigidly this was enforced is not known, but it did exist. Most of the original 13 states had similar oaths, other than Virginia, where Jefferson and Madison fought for religious freedom for all. Such oaths were banned, though, in the U.S. Constitution. As the country moved westward, fewer states had religious qualifications. Some states merely required a belief in god without any statement of what type of god was needed. Maryland did keep theirs, though, until the 1960s. In *Torasco v. Watkins*, in 1961, the U.S. Supreme Court struck down Maryland's requirement. Thus, after 1961, both at the state and federal level religious overtones were removed.

Religious practice was another thing. As many have noted, while Judaism and Catholicism have long existed in this country, those religious are not well represented in U.S. political figures. Only one Jewish person, Joe Lieberman, has been nominated for vice president on a major political ticket (he lost in the 2000 contested election), and only two Catholics, John F. Kennedy and Joe Biden, have been elected president. (Only four have been nominated by major parties, with the other nominees, Al Smith and John Kerry, coming in the 1928 and 2004 elections, respectively.) However, this is not religious law but how people treated those of other religions. While there was not a formal religious test for office in nearly all places, there was in many places a practical one.

Religious law, although not in the area of same-sex marriage, has curiously reemerged in recent years. Many politicians have claimed that Islamic law might make a comeback in the United States, and so it must be banned before it is allowed. In an interesting twist, these are sometimes the same politicians who argue that Christian religious law founded the country and should be allowed to ban same-sex marriage. Thus, Christian religious law, in these lawmakers' eyes, is okay, but Islamic religious law is not.

It should be noted that Islamic law has never been enforced in the United States other than in privately agreed contracts (where any law is allowed, generally), despite politicians' claims. One should also note that some historians suggest that at least some English law (and probably some of the law implemented as Christian religious law) is based in part on Islamic concepts brought to England by William the Conqueror.

*See also:* History and Religion; New Bills Opposing Same-Sex Marriage; Sodom and Gomorrah; 2004 Elections and Religion; 2000s, The

## Further Reading

Beauchamp, Peter W. (2011). "Misinterpreted Justice: Problems with the Use of Islamic Legal Experts in U.S. Trial Courts." *New York Law School Law Review* 55 (4): 1097–1119.

Haridan, Nurfarahin M., Ahmad F. S. Hassan, and Yusuf Karbhari. (2018). "Governance, Religious Assurance and Islamic Banks: Do Shariah Boards Effectively Serve?" *Journal of Management & Governance* 22 (4): 1015–1043.

Lemons, Katherine, and Joshua Takano Chambers-Letson. (2014). "Rule of Law: Sharia Panic and the US Constitution in the House of Representatives." *Cultural Studies* 28 (5–6): 1048–1077.

Salaymeh, Lena. (2013). "Journal of Legal Education Commodifying Islamic Law in the U.S. Legal Academy." *Journal of Legal Education* 63 (4): 640–646.

Sharpe, Emily C. (2013). "Islamic Marriage Contracts as Simple Contracts Governed by Islamic Law: A Roadmap for U.S. Courts." *Georgetown Journal of Gender & the Law* 14 (1): 189–210.

*Torasco v. Watkins*, 367 U.S. 488 (1961).

# Religious Sacraments

With religious sacraments and ceremonies, one question is, who is allowed to participate? The flip side of this might be, who is banned? Some religions do ban gay people from partaking in religious ceremonies. This entry is not concerned with which religions ban same-sex marriage (that is discussed elsewhere), but rather which religions, regardless of their stand on same-sex marriage, do not regard those in same-sex marriage as full members.

It should be noted that the individual religious unit is often more (or less) welcoming than the religion as a whole. While the church as a whole may ban gay or lesbian parishioners from becoming members, an individual church may quietly accept the member and not ask any questions. To go to the other extreme, the church as a whole may allow same-sex marriages, but those couples may be pushed to the edge of the congregation. There is a long way from not being kicked out of a religion to being treated as a full member.

One of the main sacraments being considered here is Communion. This work considers marriage separately (obviously), so Communion is one other main sacrament to be considered (obviously, most of the focus in this entry is on Christian religions). In the Catholic religion, one must both be a Catholic and be living in agreement with Catholic doctrine to receive Communion. Most Catholic churches, though, do not have any sort of control on who gets Communion, especially for the area of living in agreement with Catholic doctrine. There have been noted times in the past when certain Catholics, most notably John Kerry, were told by religious officials not to receive Communion because they were not living good Catholic lives. However, these pronouncements were more often political steps on the part of the church to speak against some issue Kerry favored (in this case abortion) rather than a way to judge Kerry's life.

In most Protestant religions, Communion is offered to all who are baptized. However, some churches do have a separate ceremony outside of the normal worship service and so limit it to only the members of that church. Others limit it to those who are baptized and regular church attendees, although that attendance and adherence (unlike the Catholic Church) does not have to be of that faith. Some allow children to partake, even if not baptized (due in part to issues of differing beliefs on when people should be baptized). Other religions are more open and allow individual parishes to decide. The Episcopal Church, for instance, requires baptism, but many individual churches allow nonbaptized people to receive Communion.

Another Catholic ceremony to consider is last rites, which sometimes includes another ceremony called extreme unction. The sacrament involved here is viaticum, which is Communion for a dying person. There is the anointing of the sick, but that must be done by a priest; viaticum can be done by a priest or a deacon. The goal according to the church is to unite the dying person with Christ. As this ceremony only has meaning to Catholics, it would only be given to a Catholic and may be denied to someone in a same-sex marriage, as the Catholic Church does not recognize such. However, as a practical matter, a priest would probably be reluctant to deny a dying person's or a family's last wish.

In non-Christian religions, there are also sacraments of sorts, but most are limited to people in that faith (which differs from Communion for those religions that have open Communion). For instance, in the Jewish religion, there is Bar Mitzvah (for boys) and Bat Mitzvah (for girls), but those are only for Jews. Marriage is another one (but that is discussed elsewhere, as noted). There are also funeral services, but, once again, in Judaism, they are only for Jews. Some religions will hold funeral services for those who are not of their faith, but there is generally not the same level of ritual for those outside of the faith.

Some other religions very often have rituals, but they are somewhat different than sacraments. Also, how the overall religion treats people in same-sex marriage greatly affects how the rituals treat them. For example, in Buddhism, there are chants for a baby during pregnancy and after birth. However, Buddhism greatly varies in terms of how LGBTQ people are treated in general, and so the treatment of those prayers would greatly vary.

Thus, some religions may deny those in same-sex marriages entry to the sacraments, ceremonies, and rituals, but the issue is of a less public nature, other than Communion. This is, of course, outside the area of marriage that is discussed throughout the book. It is also less of an issue than marriage for many people, as those who are not welcome in a religion will very often not join it. Marriage differs in that it, like a funeral, generally only occurs once in a public setting. Some people might get married a second time, but that wedding is usually less public and very often not in a church.

*See also:* Adoption; Catholic Church, The; Eastern Orthodox Church, The; Judaism

## Further Reading

Fortescue, Adrian, J. B. O'Connell, and Alcuin Reid. (2009). *The Ceremonies of the Roman Rite Described.* 15th ed. New York: Burns & Oates.

Lynch, John. (2005). "Institution and Imprimatur: Institutional Rhetoric and the Failure of the Catholic Church's Pastoral Letter on Homosexuality." *Rhetoric & Public Affairs* 8 (3): 383–303.

Marcocci, Giuseppe. (2015). "Is This Love? Same-Sex Marriages in Renaissance Rome." *Historical Reflections* 41 (2): 37.

Patrick, Dennis. (2006). "The Story of a Gay Foster Parent." *Child Welfare* 85 (2): 123–132.

Wilson, Jeff. (2012). "'All Beings Are Equally Embraced by Amida Buddha': Jodo Shinshu Buddhism and Same-Sex Marriage in the United States." *Journal of Global Buddhism* 13 (March): 31–59.

# Restaurants

Restaurants occupy a somewhat unique space in the history of same-sex marriage and religion. Unlike a church, one does not visit there weekly or have membership before its use (as most people would, and as many churches require, before getting married in a church). On the other hand, unlike a florist or a cake designer, one might not use it infrequently before a wedding, and one would probably have used it at least once, unlike most banquet halls. Restaurants are also somewhat more public than a florist or a banquet hall, as restaurants do not make most of their money off onetime events, unlike banquet halls.

Restaurants are also one of the more public venues used. After all, when diners first go to a place, they can see who the other patrons are, how they are dressed, what the food is like, and how they are treated. Few restaurants with a lot of patrons of any one group would likely discriminate against that group, if for no other reason than that it is bad business. The same could be said for a florist, but the average person is not observing 60 other floral customers when they are in a flower shop, unlike the average night in an eatery. One might not notice the other diners, but they could if they wanted to. It would be difficult to notice other customers in general in a flower shop.

However, restaurants have also been an important battleground for civil rights in the past in other contexts. The "Greensboro 4" in 1960 marked a shift in the civil rights focus, arguing against segregation at lunch counters across the South. The "whites-only" restaurants, stores, and lunch counters were areas that African Americans confronted every time they wanted to shop. Winning access to these areas was a huge part of the Civil Rights Act of 1964. Unlike civil rights protestors, gay people were generally not formally banned from restaurants. There were never laws banning gay people in general enacted by the state. There also have been fewer public bans of gay or lesbian restaurant patrons in recent years. One restaurant in Texas posted a sign saying that it was a place "where men act like men" and then refused to serve two gay men. At the time, Texas did not (and does not at the time of this writing) have any general law protecting the rights of LGBTQ individuals.

One might wonder how often there has been any discrimination against a gay man or a lesbian or a same-sex couple in a restaurant. This has occurred, as noted, but the rate of discrimination is not easy to quantify. Many such instances have occurred. For example, a South Carolina restaurant put a note calling an LGBTQ customer a slur into that customer's take-out order. While the establishment claimed to not discriminate, that message had obviously not reached the person preparing the order. One also has to wonder how public that establishment's message of equal treatment was.

All this relates to same-sex marriage in that after a marriage, one often has a reception. Before the marriage, there is often a rehearsal dinner. One does one or both in connection with a restaurant. Some restaurants have noted a desire to not serve same-sex weddings and claimed religious liberty as the reason. One such restaurant was in O'Fallon, Missouri (just west of St. Louis). Madison's Café had been the choice of two lesbians for their rehearsal dinner, as the spot had been much desired by the deceased father of one of the women. However, the eatery declined the business because the management believed that the marriage was "unhealthy." They were perfectly willing to serve the dinner until they found out who was getting married.

Other establishments have discriminated against same-sex couples earlier in the process. One place in Florida had the owner approach a lesbian couple and call them "disgusting." The owner later apologized, but only after being criticized on social media. One must wonder how many subtle acts of discrimination occur against the LGBTQ community when they try to book restaurants for reception food (or a reception) or for a rehearsal dinner if one is not familiar with the establishment (or if the owner is willing to serve LGBTQ people but not host their dinners).

One also must wonder how this all relates to religion. It does in a number of important ways. First, religion is often the claimed motivation for the anti-LGBTQ behavior on the part of the owner. Second, religion is what is often used to try to defend the establishment, either legally or morally. If it ever reaches a court, one would assume that the Religious Freedom Restoration Act (RFRA) or something similar on a state level would be invoked.

It should be noted that this entry does not discuss how restaurants must treat its employees if the employees are LGBTQ or how restaurants must treat its employees if they are in a same-sex marriage. That is very often quite different from how customers must be treated. One is an area of equal access, and the other is an area of employment law.

**See also:** *Burwell v. Hobby Lobby*; *Masterpiece Cakeshop v. Colorado Civil Rights Commission*; *Obergefell v. Hodges*; Religious Freedom Restoration Act; 2000s, The

## Further Reading

Giuffre, Patti A., and Christine L. Williams. (1994). "Boundary Lines: Labeling Sexual Harassment in Restaurants." *Gender and Society* 8 (3): 378.

Israel, Josh. (2014). "Texas Restaurant Bans Gay Couple because 'We Do Not Like Fags.'" ThinkProgress, May 29, 2014. https://thinkprogress.org/texas-restaurant-bans-gay-couple-because-we-do-not-like-fags-ac0a81703fd4/.

Ketchum, Alexandra. (2018). "'The Place We've Always Wanted to Go but Never Could Find': Finding Woman Space in Feminist Restaurants and Cafés in Ontario 1974–1982." *Feminist Studies* 44 (1): 126.

Reisner, Sari L, Jaclyn M. White Hughto, Emilia E. Dunham, Katherine J. Heflin, Jesse Blue Glass Begenyi, Julia Coffey-Esquivel, and Sean Cahill. (2015). "Legal Protections in Public Accommodations Settings: A Critical Public Health Issue for Transgender and Gender-Nonconforming People." *Milbank Quarterly* 93 (3): 484–515.

Villarreal, Daniel. (2019). "Restaurant Refuses to Host Lesbian Couple's 'Unhealthy' Wedding Rehearsal Dinner." LGBTQ Nation, June 7, 2019. https://www.lgbtqnation.com/2019/06/restaurant-refuses-host-lesbian-couples-unhealthy-wedding-rehearsal-dinner/.

# S

## Same-Sex Marriage Worldwide

Same-sex marriage worldwide varies greatly, and it is largely related to what continent one is on. In Africa and Asia, moving alphabetically, same-sex marriage is generally not allowed, and same-sex activities relations may even be criminalized. In Western Europe, on the other hand, same-sex marriage is generally legal, and the couples there enjoy the same level of rights, if not more, than in the United States. In South America and the Caribbean, change is occurring. Religion plays a role in Africa and Asia, and its absence probably plays a role in some of Europe.

Currently, it is estimated that about 30 countries, out of the more than 200 that make up the world, allow same-sex marriage. Most of those are in Europe. The only continent (other than Australia) where every country allows some form of same-sex marriage is North America, where Canada, the United States, and some places in Mexico allow it. In Africa, there is only 1 country, South Africa, which has, interestingly enough, allowed it for nearly 15 years. In Asia (and the Pacific), there are only 3 countries that allow it (Pew Research 2019).

Most of the countries that allow same-sex marriage in Europe are in Western Europe, although some in Western Europe still ban the practice. Those in Western Europe that do not allow it include Switzerland, where the reason for not allowing it is partly because Switzerland has registered partnerships, which is a couple of steps below marriage. However, the same-sex marriages were resisted (as were the partnerships, although not successfully) by political parties who were influenced by fundamentalist Christianity. Most of the rest of Western Europe allows it. In Eastern Europe, it is typically not allowed, as Russia does not allow it, and most people in public opinion polls oppose it. In Poland, another large Eastern

European country, same-sex couples who live together have been given some rights, but that is a status well below even a registered partnership.

In Africa, many nations still prohibit same-sex activity. Thus, it is not surprising that only one nation has allowed same-sex marriage, South Africa, which has a different colonial heritage than other nations. South Africa's constitution was adopted relatively late, coming in after apartheid. That document bans discrimination based on sexual orientation and was the first one in the world to do so. There was also a strong human rights campaign to end apartheid, and that influenced the treatment of LGBTQ people as well. Elsewhere in Africa, same-sex attraction is often criminalized. In five African countries, there is the death penalty for same-sex activity, and those who support LGBTQ equality in Nigeria can be punished. About 20 countries (of the 50 plus in Africa) do not ban same-sex attraction, but they do not treat it the same as heterosexuality either. Religion played a role in some countries, as the leader of the Ethiopian Orthodox Church spoke out strongly against it; that country still punishes same-sex activity with prison terms. Many leaders have also spoken out against it using religious language to justify a ban, among other justifications.

In Asia and the Pacific, only three countries allow it and only one in what is traditionally thought of as Asia. Only Taiwan allows same-sex marriage (along with Australia and New Zealand). Taiwan changed its laws to allow the practice in 2019, but only after the Judicial Yuan (somewhat parallel to the U.S. Supreme Court) ordered it to happen and ordered the Legislative Yuan (similar to the U.S. Congress) to make it happen. Referendums were passed in opposition, but the government noted that referendums could not thwart the Judicial Yuan. Among the reasons given in opposition were that some groups felt that Christianity did not allow it, and the Christian community in Taiwan was most against it. All the other nations in Asia, other than the three noted, did not allow same-sex marriage. In Pakistan, the main reason for the opposition was Islam, and those who are gay or lesbian can be punished under either Islamic law or state law. With penalties for being gay or lesbian, same-sex marriage is still far away.

In South America, moves have been made by several countries to allow for same-sex marriage, including Brazil, the largest nation by population in South America. The Caribbean has also started to be affected by change. Belize's Supreme Court has acted to decriminalize same-sex activity, which is an important first step toward equality. Tisdale wrote an article on the subject, which "concludes by recognizing that equality in the

Caribbean may be a slow process, but it is happening and most importantly, it is happening organically which is the only way to ensure long term success" (2018, 100). Thus, the Caribbean is also moving toward allowing more freedom for LGBTQ people.

Around the globe, there seem to be almost two hemispheres of treatment of same-sex marriage. One (North America, South America, and Europe) seems to have mostly decided to allow same-sex marriage. However, the other (Asia, Africa, and Oceania) seems to still be resisting same-sex marriage and has moved against marriage equality. Given the slow process of change, it will be quite a while before one world emerges on the issue.

*See also:* Catholic Church, The; Eastern Orthodox Church, The; Islam; Judaism; Religious Law and Practice in the United States Historically

## Further Reading

Merin, Yuval. (2002). *Equality for Same-Sex Couples: The Legal Recognition of Gay Partnerships in Europe and the United States*. Chicago: University of Chicago Press.

Newton, David E. (2010). *Same-Sex Marriage: A Reference Handbook*. Contemporary World Issues. Santa Barbara, CA: ABC-CLIO.

Pew Research. (2019). "Same-Sex Marriage around the World." https://www.pewforum.org/fact-sheet/gay-marriage-around-the-world/.

Pierceson, Jason, Adriana Piatti-Crocker, and Shawn Schulenberg. (2010). *Same-Sex Marriage in the Americas: Policy Innovation for Same-Sex Relationships*. Lanham, MD: Lexington Books.

Tisdale, Lauren. (2018). "A Triumphant Victory for Gay Rights in Belize Lays the Foundation for a Domino Effect throughout the Caribbean." *Loyola of Los Angeles International & Comparative Law Review* 41 (1): 99–123.

Vanita, Ruth. (2005). *Love's Rite: Same-Sex Marriage in India and the West*. London: Palgrave Macmillan.

# Sodom and Gomorrah

The story of the cities of Sodom and Gomorrah in the Bible is frequently seen as biblical backing for a variety of antigay measures. The term *sodomy* even comes, linguistically, from this. Now, why it was called "sodomy" and not "gomorrahy" is not clear. This story thus deserves a bit more attention.

The story of Sodom and Gomorrah is in the book of Genesis. The city of Sodom is where Lot, the nephew of Abraham, lived. Two angels visited Lot and protected him. However, there were not enough good people in Sodom to make the city worth saving, and so the city was destroyed with the infamous "fire and brimstone." Lot is told not to look back, but Lot's wife does and is turned into a pillar of salt.

As two entire cities (actually four, but Sodom and Gomorrah are the two remembered) were destroyed for what appears to be illicit sex, many use this story to indicate that same-sex attraction is not allowed. However, it should be noted that no explicit act is noted about what is going on in Sodom other than that the men of Sodom want to rape the two angels visiting Lot. The story also shows Lot being willing to sacrifice his two daughters by allowing the mob to rape them to save the angels, and after he left Sodom and moved into the desert, his two daughters slept with him (and the only one of the four who suffers is Lot's wife). Thus, it is apparently worse to look upon destruction than to sleep with one's father or to allow one's daughter to be raped. I am not sure most modern people who cite Sodom and Gomorrah as examples of how gay people should be punished (and same-sex marriage not allowed) are familiar with the whole story, or they do not at least realize that other people have also read the story and are opposed to the inconsistent meaning or the practices tolerated.

One should also look at what the Bible views the issue of Sodom and Gomorrah to be. The cities are mentioned numerous times. However, the same-sex activity is not the emphasis on most of those occasions. Sometimes, as might be expected, the two cities are referenced as examples of what would happen if you violated the will of God (but no mention was made of the cause of the destruction). Others passages describe the sins of the city as being adultery, lies, or generally shameless violations of God's laws. Still others say that it was the fact that the city did not welcome visitors (a mild way to describe the impending rape of the visiting angels) that caused its destruction. Arrogance is also a sin associated with the two cities. Thus, even in the times of the Bible, the same-sex nature of the cities' affairs was not what people overwhelmingly associated with Sodom and Gomorrah. That association came later.

There is also a discussion of Sodom and Gomorrah in several Jewish texts outside those preserved in the Old Testament/Torah. In those, while gay people were condemned, the people of Sodom were also guilty of a wide variety of other sins. Chief among them was a lack of hospitality. In fact, Sodom went out of its way to persecute anyone who was a foreigner. Any of those sins could have caused the destruction.

In Christian thought, there is the question of whether those in Sodom were aiming to commit rape upon Lot's visitors or were just being mean to visitors. There is also the question of what caused the destruction. Christians, similar to the views of Jews noted above, generally believed that Sodom and Gomorrah had committed a wide variety of offenses. Thus, it is entirely possible that even if Sodom were well known for its penchant toward same-sex behavior (and even if it was destroyed in fire and brimstone sent by God), the destruction could have been caused by something else.

In Islam, the destruction of Sodom is generally painted as being caused by the same-sex practices of the city.

It should be noted that the traditions of the wider Mediterranean, including Greece, generally called for kindness upon strangers. One might wonder why that would be the case. If there is no tolerance of those from other lands, no commerce occurs, and no money is made. Thus, there is a strong nonreligious reason for being kind to strangers. In Grecian religion, strangers are under the protection of the gods, and thus to harm a stranger is to violate the will of the gods. It should also be noted that all three religions, Christianity, Judaism, and Islam, call upon all people to be kind, regardless of the religion of the other. All three have a verse somewhat similar to "whoever saves one life, saves the world." Thus, Sodom, by its inhospitality, violated the social norms of at least four sets of religion (in time) and the commercial customs. It is no surprise that its destruction would be memorialized to remind others not to do the same.

One might wonder whether the cities were actually destroyed. If so, it has never been conclusively proven. It is possible, of course, that it never happened but is just a cautionary tale. While some opposed to same-sex marriage may think it is a cautionary tale against same-sex attraction, it is more likely to have been a cautionary tale against inhospitality.

***See also:*** Catholic Church, The; Chalcedon Movement; Eastern Orthodox Church, The; Islam; Judaism

## Further Reading

Ahern, Eoghan. (2018). "The Sin of Sodom in Late Antiquity." *Journal of the History of Sexuality* 2: 209.

Carlson, Reed. (2012). "The Open God of the Sodom and Gomorrah Cycle." *Journal of Pentecostal Theology* 21 (2): 185.

Cocks, H. G. (2010). "The Discovery of Sodom, 1851." *Representations* 112 (1): 1.

Gnuse, Robert K. (2015). "Seven Gay Texts: Biblical Passages Used to Condemn Homosexuality." *Biblical Theology Bulletin* 45 (2): 68.

Toensing, Holly Joan. (2005). "Women of Sodom and Gomorrah: Collateral Damage in the War against Homosexuality?" *Journal of Feminist Studies in Religion* 21 (2): 61–74.

# State Laws on Religious Freedom

The issue of state laws on religious freedom (and how they affect same-sex marriage) can be broken into two large and different parts. First, there is the question of the state constitution and all of its areas. Then there are state laws. In both, any provision cannot reduce any freedom (in religion or anywhere else) granted in the U.S. Constitution. However, freedoms can be enlarged past those in the U.S. Constitution as long as no other part of the Constitution is violated.

State constitutions have acted to both enlarge and limit one's right to marriage equality. This can be both in the area of religion and elsewhere. The most obvious example of this is when the Hawaii Constitution held that the state could not ban equality on the basis of sex, a provision not (as of the time of this writing) in the U.S. Constitution. In 1993, the Hawaii Supreme Court interpreted this to mean that same-sex marriage could not be banned. This in turn started the whole movement that led to the Defense of Marriage Act (DOMA) and eventually marriage equality nationwide. Thus, an area outside religion can affect areas that many people see religion in.

Hawaii, by the way, used the same language in the area of freedom of religion (and freedom from religion) as the U.S. Constitution. Some state constitutions have wider language on the freedom of religion. For example, Nevada's religious freedom provision reads as follows: "The free exercise and enjoyment of religious profession and worship without discrimination or preference shall forever be allowed in this State, and no person shall be rendered incompetent to be a witness on account of his opinions on matters of his religious belief, but the liberty of consciene [conscience] hereby secured, shall not be so construed, as to excuse acts of licentiousness or justify practices inconsistent with the peace, or safety of this State" (https://www.leg.state.nv.us/Const/NvConst.html). This is a bit wider than the U.S. Constitution, as it includes religious practice specifically. One case brought under Nevada's constitution dealt with another of Nevada's provisions, that public funds cannot be used for sectarian purposes, and the case challenged a school voucher program. The Nevada Supreme Court ruled that the voucher program was illegal, even though a similar voucher program had been allowed in other states.

Some also had religious restrictions, such as Maryland's test oath, which was only outlawed in 1961. Other states, some 30 of them, have constitutional provisions that ban state funds for religious "worship, exercise or instruction." This was used to ban scholarships in one state for theology, and the U.S. Supreme Court upheld this ban.

State laws can also be more kind to a religion than what is required. In *Oregon v. Smith*, the court held that a state can exempt a religion from a ban. In the *Smith* case, the question (as construed by the U.S. Supreme Court) was whether a state had to exempt Alfred Smith from a general ban on peyote use, as Smith's use was religious. The court held that Oregon could without violating the U.S. Constitution but did not have to. Many states have granted exemptions to religious organizations so that they do not have to participate in same-sex marriages, although sometimes if an area had been pledged to remain open for all, the state would force the church to open the area. However, these were based on state law rather than a state's constitutional provisions.

State laws sometimes work the other way as well. It was a state law that was used to fine Masterpiece Cakeshop (although it was a state antidiscrimination law rather than a religious freedom law) in the case that eventually went all the way to the U.S. Supreme Court. State laws on religious freedom would currently probably not be used to promote same-sex marriage. However, some churches did, before *Obergefell*, argue that state bans on same-sex marriage restricted their religious freedom.

*See also:* Loving v. Virginia; Masterpiece Cakeshop v. Colorado Civil Rights Commission; New Bills Opposing Same-Sex Marriage; 2004 Elections and Religion; *United Church of Christ v. Cooper*

## Further Reading

Davis, Derek. (2000). *Religion and the Continental Congress, 1774–1789: Contributions to Original Intent*. Religion in America Series. New York: Oxford University Press.

Lupu, Ira C. (2010). "Federalism and Faith Redux." *Harvard Journal of Law & Public Policy* 33 (3): 935.

Maroukis, Thomas Constantine. (2010). *The Peyote Road: Religious Freedom and the Native American Church*. The Civilization of the American Indian Series, Vol. 265. Norman: University of Oklahoma Press.

Nevada Constitution. https://www.leg.state.nv.us/Const/NvConst.html.

Reuben, Richard C., and L. Anita Richardson. (1997). "Supreme Court Preview: Church and State Revisited: Religious Freedom Case Raises Important Underlying Federalism Questions." *ABA Journal* 83 (3): 38.

Scaperlanda, Michael. (2007). "Symposium Issue: What about Federalism— States' Rights and the New State Immigration Laws Religious Freedom in the Face of Harsh State and Local Immigration Laws." *Tulsa Journal of Comparative and International Law* 15 (2): 165–178.

# Surrogacy

For those in same-sex marriages, surrogacy is much more important than for those in opposite-sex marriages. The reason is obvious: the only ways for same-sex couples to have kids of their own is either surrogacy or artificial insemination (unless they bring their children in from a previous opposite-sex relationship). Religion plays a role in this, as various religions have differing stands on surrogacy and artificial insemination. This in turn plays a role in state politics because some states have different stands on how a surrogate mother is treated. This entry will also discuss where states have treated opposite-sex couples different from same-sex couples in regard to these issues.

Various religions have different stands on the issue of surrogacy. The Catholic Church, for instance, opposes surrogacy, holding that it commercializes women, and points out how people around the world have been paid to participate. In an interesting twist, the church, which has not been thought of as feminist, also complains about how the practice demeans women. The Southern Baptist Convention has also condemned the practice (Klett 2019). Russell Moore suggested foster care or adoption, rather than surrogacy, and holds that it commercializes women. In both treatments, there was significant discussion of how people in the Third World have been pushed into surrogacy to make money. Little discussion took place about those in the United States who serve as surrogates.

The third-largest religion in the United States is the United Methodist Church (this is before the split that is imminent), and the fourth is the Mormons (officially titled the Church of Jesus Christ of Latter-day Saints). The Methodists do not take a definitive stand on the issue but argue that it should only be undertaken with counseling and prayer (New York State Task Force on Life and the Law 2017). The Mormons, in turn, do not allow the practice. Two other smaller U.S. religions that do allow surrogacy are Reform and Conservative Judaism, although there are notes made by both religions to make sure that the woman involved does it voluntarily. Some states have tried to regulate the practice and, in doing so, have noted that there is a wide variety of difference in the religious community on the issue.

In terms of fertility, on the other hand, that help is accepted, except by the Catholic Church and Orthodox Judaism, as long as the sperm and egg are from the couple. Some religions allow in vitro fertilization (IVF) treatment, even if the sperm and egg are not both from the couple. The idea that an embryo from both parents is better than one from one parent and a donor occurs in several religions. That, of course, creates difficulties for the same-sex couple. It is interesting to note that some churches argue that the parent needs a personal connection to the child, which argues against surrogacy, and then suggests adoptions are better (where there is generally no personal connection to the child). This is not to argue against adoptions, but just to point out a contradiction (Sallam and Sallam 2016). Few of these religions that allow same-sex marriage ban adoption for it. Or they allow same-sex marriage and surrogacy but only for opposite-sex couples. Or they allow IVF with donated sperm or a donated egg for opposite-sex couples but not for same-sex couples. In other words, it is more a package deal—surrogacy (or IVF) for all, if we (the religion) allow same-sex marriage at all.

It should be noted here that some of these same religions that favor adoption over surrogacy or IVF also oppose adoption by same-sex couples, and so there is no good option for same-sex couples according to that religion. No religion, as far as has been researched, allows same-sex marriage but opposes adoption by it. Few even allow same-sex marriage but offer no option for child-rearing. Adoption seems to be the most preferred way to bring a child into a marriage, but one must also wonder whether that is in part because it has been around longer. It should also be noted that adoption may be favored because it solves, in some people's minds, two problems: it provides a child for the childless, and it removes a child from foster care or an orphanage, neither of which is a desired location. Those are not noted religious justifications, though, and are not used by any religion, but they should still be considered as underlying thoughts.

Religions are also not quick to change, and so that must be figured into why some religions have not adapted to same-sex marriage or surrogacy or IVF. It should also be admitted that most religions base their ideas at least in part on the text of their founder or founders, and surrogacy and IVF were not around at that time. It is difficult for many religions to adapt to this. Other outcomes really should not be expected. Religions aim to provide a way of life, and if that way was adapting every day, like some sciences do, there would be no way of life provided for. This is not to say that their views are correct; these are just other factors to consider. Thus, some religions allow for IVF and surrogacy and for same-sex marriages, but opposite-sex marriages are in many ways still privileged in those religions.

*See also:* Adoption; Baptist Church, The; Catholic Church, The; Judaism; Methodists

## Further Reading

Chambers, Deborah. (2012). *A Sociology of Family Life: Change and Diversity in Intimate Relations*. Cambridge, UK: Polity Press.

Klett, Leah MarieAnn. (2019). "Russell Moore Highlights Dangers of Surrogacy, Says It 'Turns Children into a Product.'" *Christian Post*, January 21, 2019.

Markens, Susan. (2003). *Surrogate Motherhood and the Politics of Reproduction*. Berkeley: University Presses of California, Columbia, and Princeton.

Murphy, Dean A. (2015). *Gay Men Pursuing Parenthood via Surrogacy: Reconfiguring Kinship*. New South Wales, AU: UNSW Press.

New York State Task Force on Life and the Law. (2017). *Revisiting Surrogate Parenting: Analysis and Recommendations for Public Policy on Gestational Surrogacy*. New York: New York State Task Force on Life and the Law.

Rosenthal, Beth. (2013). *Gay Parenting*. Opposing Viewpoints Series. Farmington Hills, MI: Greenhaven Press.

Sallam, H. N., and N. H. Sallam. (2016). "Religious Aspects of Assisted Reproduction." *Facts, Views & Vision* 8 (1): 33–48.

Shanley, Mary Lyndon. (2002). *Making Babies, Making Families: What Matters Most in an Age of Reproductive Technologies, Surrogacy, Adoption, and Same-Sex and Unwed Parents*. Boston: Beacon Press.

# T

## 2004 Elections and Religion

In the 2004 elections, the Republican candidate, George W. Bush, openly embraced religion while the Democratic candidate, John Kerry, stayed mostly away from it, continuing a trend that started in the 1980s. John Kerry was also caught in a quagmire in that some of his coreligionists did not consider him Catholic enough. On the whole, same-sex marriage figured into the 2004 elections in a major way.

The Republican party made same-sex marriage a major talking point. George W. Bush, the sitting president, had pushed for a constitutional amendment to ban it (thus turning the Defense of Marriage Act (DOMA) into a permanent part of the U.S. Constitution), but that failed. However, he still supported the issue in the 2004 elections. The issue had also started to heat up at the time, with Massachusetts becoming the first state in that year to legalize it. Kerry was from Massachusetts, having served as its lieutenant governor and senator, and so he was tied to the issue. The Democratic candidate favored equal rights for gay individuals, but he also downplayed it, focusing more on causes he felt were winnable. While one might condemn Kerry based on current attitudes, in 2004, only the one state had marriage equality. Bush aimed to win and thus had both his beliefs and his political prospects aligned.

The two political parties generally aligned with their leaders. The Republican platform argued for traditional marriage and railed against judges. The platform stated, "In some states, activist judges are redefining the institution of marriage" ("Republican National Platform" 2004). The Democratic platform simply held that it was a state issue and only mentioned marriage twice (the Republican platform had mentioned it 19 times). The Democratic platform stated, "In our country, marriage has been defined at the state level for 200 years, and we believe it should continue to be defined there" ("Democratic National Platform" 2004). The Republicans thus tried to keep marriage front and center in the federal elections.

It should be noted that Kerry had supported other LGBTQ issues, including the service of gay and lesbian people in the military, but these issues did not receive nearly the prominence of marriage equality. Part of this may have been due to the fact that the federal government had already allowed "Don't Ask, Don't Tell" (DADT), which the Republicans said was working, and it was somewhat difficult to maneuver in that area to create a clear difference between DADT and full open service. The 2004 Democratic platform also avoided discussion of the issue, while the Republican platform called for a move back to pre-DADT days.

On the whole, same-sex marriage caused problems for Kerry. Campbell and Monson noted, "On the other hand, the issue of gay marriage seemed to stymie the Kerry campaign, caught between not wanting to alienate the socially liberal base of the Democratic Party and recognizing that outright support for gay marriage is controversial among the general public" (Campbell and Monson 2008, 401). Kerry's unclear position may have cost him some support. At the very least, it caused him to run a weaker overall campaign than otherwise.

Kerry also had other religious issues in the race. Kerry was a Catholic, and previous Catholic presidential candidates had had to deal with the issue of the pope having too much power in U.S. elections if the president was Catholic. This was not an issue here but quite the opposite. Many argued that Kerry was not Catholic enough and that he was not even in good standing with the church (an issue that had not really come up that often in previous elections or since). Kerry held for the separation of church and state. This got him in hot water with the Catholic Church, as he would not want to ban abortion, even though he was personally opposed to it. In turn, at least one archbishop of the church said that they would deny him Communion, and he received an official letter warning him that he was a heretic. Some postelection analyses have Bush winning over 50 percent of the Catholic vote, which hurt Kerry at the polls and may have cost him some states.

Other than those two issues, religion did not directly enter the 2004 election. Many supported George W. Bush for religious reasons, but most of those voters would have probably supported any Republican candidate. People of other religious views supported Kerry, but the same would probably have supported any Democratic candidate.

Both issues (same-sex marriage and his Catholicism, or lack thereof) received a fair amount of national airtime, but nationwide, same-sex marriage probably hurt Kerry's chances more. On that issue, the Democratic party was ahead of its time; the second state to adopt gay marriage was Connecticut, but that was four years later, and the first state to have the voters adopt it was in 2012, a full eight years after the election. By 2015, the U.S. Supreme Court had declared that the U.S. Constitution requires marriage equality, and the nation largely accepted the decision. There had been a great shift in public opinion in that time period.

*See also:* Buttigieg, Pete; *Masterpiece Cakeshop v. Colorado Civil Rights Commission*; *Obergefell v. Hodges*; 2000s, The; *United States v. Windsor*

## Further Reading

Campbell, David E. (2007). *A Matter of Faith: Religion in the 2004 Presidential Election*. Washington, DC: Brookings Institution Press.

Campbell, David E., and J. Quin Monson. (2008). "The Religion Card: Gay Marriage and the 2004 Presidential Election." *Public Opinion Quarterly* 72 (3): 399.

"Democratic National Platform." (2004). American Presidency Project, University of California Santa Barbara. https://www.presidency.ucsb.edu/documents /2004-democratic-party-platform.

Dulio, David A., and Candice J. Nelson. (2005). *Vital Signs: Perspectives on the Health of American Campaigning*. Washington, DC: Brookings Institution Press.

Green, John C. (2007). *The Faith Factor: How Religion Influences American Elections*. Religion, Politics, and Public Life. Westport, CT: Greenwood Publishing Group.

"Republican National Platform." (2004). American Presidency Project, University of California Santa Barbara. https://www.presidency.ucsb.edu/documents /2004-republican-party-platform.

Smith, Daniel A., Matthew DeSantis, and Jason Kassel. (2006). "Same-Sex Marriage Ballot Measures and the 2004 Presidential Election." *State & Local Government Review* 38 (2): 78–91.

# 2000s, The

The 2000s saw increasingly heated battles waged between religious institutions and advocates of LGBTQ rights. Forces on both sides had been awakened in the 1980s and 1990s with the rise of conservative religious forces in a movement self-titled the "Moral Majority" and the subsequent LGBTQ rights movement. The first decade of the second millennium saw these forces clash.

The 2000s saw the issue of same-sex marriage come to the forefront. In the 1990s, a few states considered giving some level of marriage rights to same-sex couples, but it was only a few. The issue was first thrust in front of the public by the Hawaii Supreme Court's ruling from the 1990s that its state constitution supported same-sex marriages. By the end of the 2000s, nearly every state had taken some action, with battles within each state between those supporting and opposing same-sex marriages. However, other religious and political forces also joined the fray.

Many religions had to grapple with how their doctrines viewed same-sex attraction and whether their overall worldview adequately addressed the issue. Among those most in opposition of bans on same-sex marriage were the Unitarian Universalists, while the Church of Jesus Christ of Latter-day Saints (the Mormons) and the Catholic Church fought in favor of the bans. Other churches had to maneuver through the opinions of their members. The Presbyterian Church USA (PC(USA)), which is the largest Presbyterian denomination, struggled over the issue. In 1994, for instance, it passed language holding that one had to either live singly or in a marriage between a man and a woman. In the 2000s, it again debated the issue, and in 2008, it voted to start removing barriers to ordination and officership for gay church members. Thus, many denominations represented a range of opinions on the issue, and some moved over time.

One of the first battlegrounds for same-sex marriage in the 2000s was Massachusetts, where the Massachusetts Supreme Court declared that the state needed to have marriage equality. The Catholic Church, a force powerful in both religion and politics there, was among those mobilized against the ruling. Other religious forces, including the Unitarian Universalist Church, welcomed it. A third group, including Governor Mitt Romney, stated that they would abide by the court's decision even while not agreeing, occupying a middle ground. Those opposed, including the Catholic Church, tried to push for a constitutional convention in the state to force a rewritten state constitution. In this way, they hoped to avoid seeing the effects of the state supreme court's decision. However, their efforts fell short, and the state constitution remained unchanged. The decision's effects extended "well past the geographical boundaries of the Commonwealth of Massachusetts" in many ways, particularly as the decision came with "new obligations on the part of employers to provide benefits to the workforce" (Ashton and Feldman 2004, 11).

Religious forces were also grappling with LGBTQ advocates in California. An initiative implemented in 2000 created a state law banning same-sex marriage. However, in 2008, that law was struck down as contrary to the state constitution. As in Massachusetts, opponents of same-sex marriage then took aim at the state constitution itself with Proposition 8, which sought to amend the state constitution to ban same-sex marriage. Proposition 8 was strongly supported by the Catholic Church and the Church of Jesus Christ of Latter-day Saints. Those two forces united, and the Latter-day Saints produced a letter to be read in every congregation. The Orthodox Jewish communities in California along with the Eastern Orthodox Church also favored the ban.

However, not all religious forces favored Proposition 8. The Episcopal Church came out strongly against it. Several Jewish groups did as well, being mostly Reformed and Conservative Jewish organizations. As elsewhere, the Unitarian Universalists strongly opposed the effort and supported same-sex marriage. Thus, there was a battle between various religious fronts as well as outside of the religious realm. Ultimately, Proposition 8 was passed, and the California State Constitution was amended to ban same-sex marriage. Subsequently, the U.S. Supreme Court upheld a lower court ruling on a technical basis, which effectively upheld Proposition 8, and this ended the issue in California until it returned at the national level.

The 2000s also saw a host of other issues for same-sex couples, married or not, including how they were seen as potential adoptive parents: "Second-parent adoption has proved a powerful legal device for gay and lesbian families. It is modeled on step-parent adoption, a statutory scheme that allows a biological (or adoptive) parent's spouse to adopt a child without terminating that parent's rights, thereby leaving the child with two parents. However critical this method of securing the family's legal protection remains—and will remain for the foreseeable future—there is a conceptual flaw in analogizing same-sex couples to a step-family" (Polikoff 2009, 205). When a second parent in a same-sex union wanted to adopt a child, that parent was forced to use a legal code that was designed for blended families. Although the code did allow the adoption to progress, it left much to be desired in regard to true equality.

The first decade of the 21st century represented a key turning point in the debate over same-sex marriage and religion. In the wake of increasing state legislation on same-sex marriage, each religion needed to decide how to treat gay and lesbian couples who wanted to wed. Churches also had to decide whether their views were going to influence public policy. The religions generally agreed that, yes, their views should influence public policy, but they disagreed on how best to enact public policy. These internal battles continued into the second decade, which saw the United States legally adopt marriage across the land.

*See also:* Generational Differences; Mormons; Presbyterians; 2004 Elections and Religion; United Kingdom

## Further Reading

Ashton, Judith, and Gary M. Feldman. (2004). "The Massachusetts Same-Sex Marriage Ruling: Groundbreaking Issues in the American Workplace." *Employee Relations Law Journal* 30 (3): 3–13.

Gill, Emily R. (2012). *An Argument for Same-Sex Marriage: Religious Freedom, Sexual Freedom, and Public Expressions of Civic Equality*. Religion and Politics Series. Washington, DC: Georgetown University Press.

Jones, Robert P. (2016). *The End of White Christian America*. New York: Simon & Schuster.

Laycock, Douglas, Anthony R. Picarello, and Robin Fretwell Wilson. (2008). *Same-Sex Marriage and Religious Liberty: Emerging Conflicts*. Washington, DC: Beckett Fund for Religious Liberty.

Pierceson, Jason, Adriana Piatti-Crocker, and Shawn Schulenberg. (2010). *Same-Sex Marriage in the Americas: Policy Innovation for Same-Sex Relationships*. Lanham, MD: Lexington Books.

Polikoff, Nancy D. (2009). "A Mother Should Not Have to Adopt Her Own Child: Parentage Laws for Children of Lesbian Couples in the Twenty-First Century." *Stanford Journal of Civil Rights & Civil Liberties* 5 (2): 201–268.

Viefhues-Bailey, Ludger H. (2010). *Between a Man and a Woman? Why Conservatives Oppose Same-Sex Marriage*. Gender, Theory, and Religion. New York: Columbia University Press.

# U

## United Church of Christ v. Cooper

When most people think of lawsuits that pitch a church versus the state in the area of same-sex marriage, they picture a church opposing same-sex marriage while the state has come to favor it. That is the case in the post *Obergefell* world, of course, as all states have legalized the practice of same-sex marriage. However, before *Obergefell*, not every state favored same-sex marriage and not all churches opposed it, and some lawsuits resulted from this. One was this case, *United Church of Christ* (or *UCC*) *v. Cooper*, which came out of North Carolina.

Here, the United Church of Christ (UCC) wanted to marry same-sex couples, but the state of North Carolina did not. So the UCC sued the governor, Roy Cooper, resulting in the name of the case. There were three different groups that joined in the lawsuit, those being the church itself, the ministers, and the people wanting to get married. The groups argued collectively that their right to marriage equality was being denied by the state's decision to not allow same-sex couples to be married. The involvement of the churches and the ministers is a step past what was seen with interracial marriage, which had generally just involved the people being married and the state (of course, interracial marriage also generally involved a prison term, whereas such was not usually imposed in the case of same-sex marriage).

The case was filed in April 2014, with a temporary and then a permanent injunction being granted. The injunction held that as the U.S. Fourth Circuit, which covers North Carolina, was hearing a case (*Bostic*) that dealt with the same issues, an injunction was justified until the Fourth Circuit ruled. Once the Fourth Circuit held that there was a right to marriage equality, the injunction then became permanent. Finally, the U.S. Supreme Court held in *Obergefell* that there was a right to marriage equality nationwide, which ended the issue as far as the courts were concerned. The case was then dismissed, other than arguing over attorney fees, which, of course, was important and, not surprisingly, took quite a while.

The issue at hand was then dealt with, but the question still remained of how religious objections should still be dealt with in terms of when churches are more pro–marriage equality than the state itself. The *Cooper* case definitely held that the church and the ministers had standing to challenge the rule. Thus, it was more than just the typical state versus person dispute that has been seen elsewhere.

One might ask why a church would have standing to challenge a rule like North Carolina's marriage ban, but the answer was that the ban was telling the church who it could and could not marry. Similarly, it was telling ministers whom they could and could not marry. This restricted the religious freedom of churches and ministers, and one of the clear rules of the First Amendment was that the state could not tell religious officials what to do. One might ask whether a church or a minister on the other side of the debate (who opposed marriage equality) could sue to defend North Carolina's ban, and the answer would be no, as lifting the ban did not order any church to perform same-sex marriages but merely allowed it.

Looking forward, how might this decision (and the ideas behind it, as a district court decision by itself is not that shaping) mold the future of same-sex marriage? First, it points out how unlikely allies can arise to promote marriage equality. Few would have expected in the early 2010s to have a church and its ministers work together with same-sex couples for equality. It also points out how religious opinion is by no means monolithic, even among those motivated enough to come to court. Those forces opposing marriage equality may get most of the press, but there were also those forces that favored marriage equality and were interested enough to wind up in the courtroom.

However, will a state regulation likely be challenged in this way again? It is less likely than before. Short of a state ban on marriage equality in church policies or a state regulation requiring different treatment by a church, it is difficult to see how a church would sue. A state may allow a church, under religious freedom, to treat two groups differently, but that would not allow a church favoring marriage equality to sue against that practice. Thus, this case reveals the variety of opinions and holds that not all churches in the courts were opposed to marriage equality, but this may be of less consequence moving forward.

*See also:* Evangelicals; *Obergefell v. Hodges*; Religious Law and Practice in the United States Historically; State Laws on Religious Freedom; 2000s, The

## Further Reading

Goldstein, Warren. (2004). *William Sloane Coffin, Jr.: A Holy Impatience*. New Haven, CT: Yale University Press.

Kazyak, Emily. (2011). "Same-Sex Marriage in a Welcoming World: Rights Consciousness of Heterosexuals in Liberal Religious Institutions." *Sexuality Research & Social Policy: Journal of NSRC* 8 (3): 192.

Peay, Steven A. (2009). "Congregationalism in the United States: A Brief Overview." *International Congregational Journal* 8 (1): 61–69.

Scheitle, Christopher P., Stephen M. Merino, and Andrew Moore. (2010). "On the Varying Meaning of 'Open and Affirming.'" *Journal of Homosexuality* 57 (10): 1223–1236.

Talge, Jordan. (2010). "No Direction Home: Constitutional Limitations on Washington's Homeless Encampment Ordinances." *Washington Law Review* 85 (4): 781–813.

# United Kingdom

Same-sex marriage in the United Kingdom might seem to be an unrelated topic to the United States, but the topics are related in at least a couple of important ways. First, the United States is historically related to the United Kingdom more than any other country, as the United Kingdom had the most colonial impact. Second, in many ways, the United States modeled most of its legal system on the United Kingdom. Thus, if we are to look at any other country for its opinion on same-sex marriage (rather than looking at the world as a whole, which is covered elsewhere), the United Kingdom (which was the formal name of the union of Britain with a number of other countries in the early 18th century) is the place to look.

The United Kingdom did not set marriage policy at the level of the whole country; instead, it allowed Scotland, Ireland, and the other countries to set their own policies. Each country adopted marriage equality at a different time, but not over a long time period. The first were England and Wales in 2014, and the last was Northern Ireland in 2020. Thus, it only took the United Kingdom 6 years as opposed to the 20 or so (if you count

Hawaii's attempts in the 1990s) in the United States. The United Kingdom did have civil partnerships before, and this helped public opinion somewhat become used to the concept of same-sex partnerships in some form.

In terms of religion, the Church of England is the official church of the United Kingdom, but religious diversity is allowed. Religious bodies have a variety of opinion on the issue, with Unitarians, Quakers, and some Jews allowing for it and Muslims and Catholics opposing it. Opinions are still developing though, as the Scottish Episcopal Church changed its opinion on the issue in the 2010s while it was being legalized. Other bodies are more shaped by their worldwide church. For example, Methodists have had same-sex commitment ceremonies, but they do not call it marriage in the United Kingdom, as their worldwide governing body does not allow that (as of the time of this writing). Religious groups were also protected in the United Kingdom from having to perform same-sex marriages, and ministers were allowed to opt out even if their religion allowed it.

Public opinion also shifted relatively rapidly on the issue. In the 1980s, most people in the United Kingdom opposed same-sex attraction, but by the 2010s, most were accepting of it. With that shift came a more positive view of same-sex marriage as well. Similar to other areas (and similar to the United States), those who were young had the highest level of support, with those who were in the 60s and older having the lowest level of support. It should be noted that between civil partnerships and marriage, the public generally favored having one or the other (versus no recognition at all) by an 80–20 majority (meaning 80% wanted some recognition).

As noted, the United Kingdom adopted marriage equality on a rolling basis, with some areas (mostly small islands in the Caribbean) still having not adopted it. About five Caribbean islands that are still Crown dependencies, to use the legal term, do not recognize same-sex marriage. However, most of the main population areas have adopted it. It is less of a topic, not surprisingly, in the United Kingdom than other issues, such as Brexit, as Brexit affects everyone.

Religious opposition in the United Kingdom was also presented differently than it was in the United States. Religious groups who opposed same-sex marriage often used more secular language rather than religious. One author wrote, "While religious attitudes to same-sex marriage are closely linked to theological issues, religious opposition to the proposals of the Scottish and Westminster governments has been notable for its limited use of theological justifications. For the most part, specifically religious reasons for opposition to same-sex marriage have been altogether absent, or have been significantly downplayed in public presentations of the oppositional case. Instead, this has centered primarily on secular arguments based on tradition, social utility, democratic values and the threat to religious freedoms and liberties" (Kettell 2013, 248).

This treatment in the United Kingdom is due in part to a different role of the church in there than in United States and to the different place of the church. The church has not been at the center of the public sphere in England in the same way that it has been in the United States, and so it is not surprising that religious issues are less important. Religious holidays are also given less prominence, with no U.S. equivalent to the British bank holiday.

***See also:*** Catholic Church, The; Episcopalians; History and Religion; Religious Law and Practice in the United States Historically; Same-Sex Marriage Worldwide

## Further Reading

Eekelaar, John. (2014). "Perceptions of Equality: The Road to Same-Sex Marriage in England and Wales." *International Journal of Law, Policy & the Family* 28 (1): 1–25.

Haldane, John. (2012). "Same-Sex Marriage? A View from across the Atlantic." *Nova et Vetera* (English Edition) 10 (3): 649.

Kettell, Steven. (2013). "I Do, Thou Shalt Not: Religious Opposition to Same-Sex Marriage in Britain." *Political Quarterly* 84 (2): 247–255.

Lennox, Corinne, and Matthew Waites. (2013). *Human Rights, Sexual Orientation and Gender Identity in the Commonwealth: Struggles for Decriminalisation and Change.* London: Human Rights Consortium, School of Advanced Study.

Wilson, Kath. (2014). "The Road to Equality: The Struggle of Gay Men and Lesbians to Achieve Equal Rights before the Law." *British Journal of Community Justice* 12 (3): 81–92.

# United States v. Windsor

The question in *United States v. Windsor* was whether the Defense of Marriage Act (DOMA) covered federal law and was constitutional. *Windsor* might be seen as an unusual case to challenge the federal government's same-sex marriage treatment, as one spouse was already dead and the case dealt with the inheritance tax, a subject that does not always inspire passion like that exposed in clashing protests on same-sex marriage. In *Windsor*, a spouse wanted to avoid paying the tax, but the federal government said that she was not married and so was subject to the full tax (spouses received a sizable exemption). The case went all the way up the U.S. Supreme Court.

In many ways, although unexpected, *Windsor* demonstrates why the issue of marriage equality is so important. *Marriage* was argued to be only a word for those opposed to marriage equality. However, those wanting marriage equality pointed out that one's marital status greatly shaped federal (and state) law, in everything from the adoption of babies to one's natural death (and beyond, as shown here). *Windsor* demonstrates how true this was, as most people want to leave an estate for their loved ones (and their relatives, often, when the two are not the same group), and one person most loved in most families is the spouse of the deceased. Once again, DOMA was telling gay and lesbian people that their love was not deserving of equality, as they could not effectively leave the same amount of after-tax money. (This is not intended to take a position on whether there should be an estate tax, but just to note that if there is one, it should treat same-sex married couples and opposite-sex married couples the same.)

In this case, a New York couple, Edith Windsor and Thea Spyer, had been married in Canada, and the State of New York recognized the marriage. When Spyer died, she left her whole estate to Windsor. However, the federal government refused the marriage exemption for Spyer's estate. Windsor sued, and while the case was in the appeals process, the U.S. government dropped its support for DOMA. However, another group of defendants, who titled themselves the Bipartisan Legal Advisory Group (BLAG) (and who represented the House of Representatives), intervened and defended the bill. The court allowed this, even though the legislative branch is not usually allowed to intervene and take over the executive's role of defending a law. One suspects that the courts throughout felt it was time to rule on DOMA and that this was a good case to squarely take it on.

The court, however, sidestepped the general question of whether marriage equality was required nationwide. Instead, it focused on the discriminatory impact of a law upon a state-allowed class. The state allowed the marriages, and the court found that the federal government was not allowed to discriminate against a state-allowed class. Therefore, DOMA was struck down in federal law. The court did not go so far as to force one state to recognize marriages allowed in another, but the federal government cannot discriminate. The requirement of equal protection means that those in same-sex marriages, where legal, must be treated the same as opposite-sex marriages.

Not everyone agreed. Four justices, including Justice Scalia, dissented. Scalia had been arguing against same-sex marriage for quite some time, and this opinion was no different. Scalia argued that the case should not have been decided and that DOMA should not have been struck down. He first argued that since the executive and the estate both agreed that the tax should not have been applied, this case should not have been decided by the U.S. Supreme Court. (He ignores, however, that both the executive and the estate thought that DOMA was wrong, and so not deciding the case would have just ignored the issue for a short time.)

Chief Justice Roberts dissented (in addition to joining part of Scalia's dissent) and held that since DOMA was constitutionally passed, it should be allowed, and since there was no proof that Congress acted with malice, the act should have been allowed. Roberts finally noted that DOMA as a whole (not just as it applied to federal law, which is the key point here) was not in front of the Supreme Court, nor was the question of whether same-sex marriage as a whole was allowed.

Finally, Justice Alito wrote a dissent. Alito said the BLAG was right to interfere, but there was no right to a same-sex marriage in the Constitution. Because of this, DOMA should have been allowed in this instance. Same-sex marriage was held to a be new right and so should have been approached with caution, which Alito did not see the U.S. Supreme Court doing in this decision.

Thus, the dissents would have put, generally, same-sex marriage at the center, which would have allowed their victory (as Kennedy probably would not have gone along with it), while the majority saw disparate treatment of those in a state that allowed same-sex marriage as the key issue.

*See also:* Defense of Marriage Act, The; Governmental Benefits; *Masterpiece Cakeshop v. Colorado Civil Rights Commission*; *Obergefell v. Hodges*; 2000s, The

## Further Reading

Bower, Chris. (2014). "Juggling Rights and Utility: A Legal and Philosophical Framework for Analyzing Same-Sex Marriage in the Wake of *United States v. Windsor*." *California Law Review* 102 (4): 971.

Civins, Kimberly E., and Tiffany N. McKenzie. (2015). "Marriage, Death and Taxes: The Estate Planning Impact of *Windsor* and *Obergefell* on Georgia's Same-Sex Spouses." *Georgia Bar Journal* 21 (2): 9.

Entin, Jonathan L. (2014). "The Supreme Court's Treatment of Same-Sex Marriage in *United States v. Windsor* and *Hollingsworth v. Perry*: Analysis and Implications." *Case Western Reserve Law Review* 64 (3): 823–828.

Naylor, Lorenda, and J. Haulsee. (2014). "Equal Treatment under the Law: A Cost-Benefit Analysis of Same-Sex Benefits Post-*Windsor*." *Journal of Health and Human Services Administration* 37 (2): 207.

Oleske, James M., Jr. (2016). "The Evolution of Accommodation: Comparing the Unequal Treatment of Religious Objections to Interracial and Same-Sex Marriages." *Dukeminier Awards Best Sexual Orientation and Gender Identity Law Review* 50: 99–152.

# Annotated Bibliography

**Badgett, M. V. Lee. (2009).** *When Gay People Get Married: What Happens When Societies Legalize Same-Sex Marriage.* **New York: New York University Press.**
This book serves as a summary of the research in 2009. It also gives a perspective of what was being presented academically about halfway into the marriage debate, between when Massachusetts allowed same-sex marriage in 2004 and *Obergefell* in 2015. It shows that the calm voices were clearly proving that there was no threat to marriage from marriage equality. This differs from some of the religious voices that were being shrill. Badgett notes that marriage of any couple changes them more than they change marriage and that marriage is beneficial to same-sex couples. Badgett is a professor of economics at the University of Massachusetts Amherst.

**Bengtsson, Niklas. (2019).** **"Are Religions for Sale? Evidence from the Swedish Church Revolt over Same-Sex Marriage."** *Journal for the Scientific Study of Religion*, **WILEY 58 (2): 336–359.**
This is one journal article that looks fully and solely at the effect of same-sex marriage on religion. It is not about a U.S. church but churches in Sweden. It examines whether the state can push a church into supporting same-sex marriage. It finds that in some cases there was what Bengtsson calls "clerical opportunism." Bengtsson is a senior lecturer in the Department of Economics at Uppsala University in Sweden.

**Cleves, Rachel Hope. (2014).** *Charity and Sylvia: A Same-Sex Marriage in Early America.* **New York: Oxford University Press.**
Cleves examines two early Americans who openly lived together for 40 years as husband and wife, or as near as they could at the time. Charity and Sylvia lived in Weybridge, Vermont, in the early 1800s. They operated a

business, served in their church, and were accepted in their community, even while their sexuality was not openly discussed. Of interest regarding the intersection of religion and same-sex unions, the pair were very active in their church. Cleves is a professor of history at the University of Victoria in Canada.

**Corvino, John, and Maggie Gallagher. (2012).** *Debating Same-Sex Marriage.* **New York: Oxford University Press.**
This book is an unusual pairing that brings together two authors from different sides of the spectrum. John Corvino is a gay rights activist and professor at Wayne State University, and Maggie Gallagher is a founder of the National Organization for Marriage and a columnist. The book allows both sides to present their views (as of 2012) and then allows both to have a rebuttal. Religion played an important role in Gallagher's stand, and so this book is important for this volume. It also provides a good reasoned sense of what the two sides of the issue were in 2012, three years before *Obergefell*.

**Eskridge, William N., Jr., and Darren R. Spedale. (2006).** *Gay Marriage: For Better or for Worse? What We've Learned from the Evidence.* **New York: Oxford University Press.**
This book looks at the actual experience of same-sex marriage (then called "gay marriage" by the authors here) in some Scandinavian countries in the first 15 or so years after its adoption. The authors argue that marriage was not harmed in the countries that adopted it, and that children are not harmed. Families, couples, and communities are all looked at. In importance for this book, the volume also looks at the effect on the churches. Eskridge is a professor at Yale Law School, and Spedale is an investment banker who spent a Fulbright researching the topic in these Scandinavian countries.

**Feit, Mario. (2011).** *Democratic Anxieties: Same-Sex Marriage, Death, and Citizenship.* **Lanham, MD: Lexington Books.**
This book looks at what it means to be a citizen and how that relates to the issue of same-sex marriage. It also ties into issues of religion, as citizenship has been related to one's religion (or lack thereof) in the past. Feit examines, among others, Rousseau, Arendt, and Nietzsche. Many argue about whether same-sex marriage was American, and Feit widens the

question to one generally of citizenship and to what extent reproduction is needed for citizenship. Feit is a professor of political science at Georgia State University.

**Ferguson, Gary. (2016).** *Same-Sex Marriage in Renaissance Rome: Sexuality, Identity, and Community in Early Modern Europe*. **Ithaca, NY: Cornell University Press.**
This book looks at same-sex marriages in Rome. Apparently, a church started holding same-sex marriages, which in turn started a trial. While the whole record of the trial does not exist, a partial one does. Between the transcript and other primary sources, Ferguson paints a fairly good picture of the events. He argues that there were same-sex marriages in the 1500s, some four centuries before any culture formally allowed it. This, like other sources, points out that same-sex marriage was desirable for some a long time ago and that, as in this case, it may have been the state rather than the church that stopped it. Ferguson is a professor of French at the University of Virginia.

**Frank, Walter. (2014).** *Law and the Gay Rights Story: The Long Search for Equal Justice in a Divided Democracy*. **New Brunswick, NJ: Rutgers University Press.**
Frank looks at the important legal cases up to 2013. Of importance, he makes complex legal topics understandable for the average nonlegal person. If someone is wanting a way into these cases at above a basic level, this is a good book to start with. Frank has written a number of different books, including *Do We Have a Center*, published in 2019, and he worked as an attorney for the Port Authority of New York for 30 years.

**Gerstmann, Evan. (2017).** *Same-Sex Marriage and the Constitution*. **3rd ed. Cambridge, UK: Cambridge University Press.**
Gerstmann's book examines the 2015 *Obergefell v. Hodges* decision. It explains the legal reasoning and what the focus on fundamental rights means. It also notes how the case was broader than just holding that the ban on same-sex marriage or its recognition was irrational or based on discrimination. Gerstmann's book follows up on his two earlier editions, published in 2008 and 2002, respectively. The author is a professor of political science at Loyola Marymount University in Los Angeles, California, and has published widely.

**Gill, Emily R. (2012).** *An Argument for Same-Sex Marriage: Religious Freedom, Sexual Freedom, and Public Expressions of Civic Equality.* **Religion and Politics Series. Washington, DC: Georgetown University Press.**

Gill presents an argument for the right to marry who one wants based on the same freedom principles as religious freedom. People have religious freedom so that they can worship the way they want to, Gill argues, and so for the same reason, they should have the right to marry whom they want. As marriage is not a religious institution in the United States, when the state says that one person is not allowed to marry the partner they choose but another can, the state is making one person less equal, which violates the idea of America as well. Gill is a chaired professor of political science at Bradley University in Illinois.

**Gozemba, Patricia, and Karen Khan. (2007).** *Courting Equality: A History of America's First Same-Sex Marriages.* **Boston, MA: Beacon Press.**

This book looks at the early families who married in Massachusetts after that state became the first to allow same-sex marriages. It points out the arguments on both sides before the marriages. The work also notes that the marriages show how love and commitment have been important for same-sex couples, just like they have always been for opposite-sex couples. It includes photographs by Marilyn Humphries. Patricia Gozemba is a former professor of English and women's studies at Salem State University and a founding member of the History Project. Karen Khan is a former editor of *Sojourner: The Women's Forum.*

**Johnson, Paul James, Robert Vanderbeck, and Silvia Falcetta. (2017).** *Religious Marriage of Same-Sex Couples: A Report on Places of Worship in England and Wales Registered for the Solemnization of Same-Sex Marriage.* **London: University of York and University of Leeds.**

This book looks at opportunities in the United Kingdom for same-sex couples to be married in a religious setting. It notes that 28 percent of opposite-sex couples still marry in the church, and it analyzed a data set to see that only 0.5 percent of same-sex couples had. Similarly, about 99.5 percent of churches in the United Kingdom do not allow same-sex marriage. This is a data-driven approach. Johnson is a professor of sociology at the University of York. Vanderbeck is a professor of geography at the University of

Leeds. Falcetta works at the University of York in the Department of Sociology.

**Kaplan, Roberta. (2015).** *Then Comes Marriage: How Two Women Fought for and Won Equal Dignity for All.* **New York: Norton.**
One might think from the title that this book is about the *Obergefell* decision. However, it is about a decision that occurred two years before that—the *Windsor* case. The *Windsor* case led to the striking down of the Defense of Marriage Act (DOMA), which basically moved the marriage equality battle nationwide. Before *Windsor*, one did not have to respect another state's marriage status, but after it, they did. This forced the court to soon face square on the issue of marriage equality. Kaplan was the attorney for *Windsor* and so brings professional and personal knowledge to the table here.

**Kimport, Katrina. (2014).** *Queering Marriage: Challenging Family Formation in the United States.* **New Brunswick, NJ: Rutgers University Press.**
Many books look at the process by which gay and lesbian couples gained the right to marry. Kimport accepts that as a given and looks at why people chose to marry. For this book, she interviewed a large number of people in San Francisco who married in 2004, in the brief period when that city offered marriage certificates in violation of state law. The book argues that some same-sex couples wanted to gain the benefits available from marriage, while others wanted to marry to argue against opposite-sex couples gaining more power due to their being heterosexual. Kimport is a professor at the University of California at San Francisco.

**Lahey, Kathy, and Kevin Alderson. (2004).** *Same-Sex Marriage: The Personal and the Political.* **Toronto: Insomniac Press.**
This book looks at same-sex marriage in those areas where it existed in 2004. It also looks at stories from other countries. Lahey is a lawyer in Canada who sued to make sure that marriage equality existed. She won in 2003. Alderson is a counselor and psychologist who specializes in studying human sexuality and has counseled thousands of LGBTQ people.

**Laycock, Douglas, Anthony R. Picarello, and Robin Fretwell Wilson, eds. (2008).** *Same-Sex Marriage and Religious Liberty: Emerging*

*Conflicts*. **Washington, DC: Beckett Fund for Religious Liberty; Rowman & Littlefield Publishers.**

This book is somewhat dated, but it represents the results of a large conference organized in 2008 on the issue. It looks at a lot of the policy options that were available at the time about same-sex marriage and how they might conflict with religion. The book is about 300 pages long and contains essays from a wide variety of contributors. Laycock was a professor of law at the University of Michigan. Picarello is the counsel for the Conference of Catholic Bishops. Wilson was a professor of law at Washington and Lee University.

**Lee, Jess. (2018). "Black LGB Identities and Perceptions of Same-Sex Marriage."** *Journal of Homosexuality: The Impact of Same-Sex Marriage on LGBTQ Activism, Politics, Communities, and Identities* **65 (14): 2005–2027.**

This article looks at how the issue of race shapes the question of same-sex marriage. It looks at how Black people who are LGBTQ view the issue. It used many different surveys and found a wide variety of views on the issue. Lee is a PhD student in sociology at the University of California at Irvine.

**Li, Anqi, and Dean Smith. (2012).** *Uses of History in the Press and in Court during California's Battle over Proposition 8: Casting Same-Sex Marriage as a Civil Right.* **New York: Mellen.**

This book looks at how history was used during the battle over Proposition 8 in 2010. In that year, there was a long federal district court trial over the proposition in the case *Hollingsworth v. Perry*. Three newspapers were examined along with a selection of court documents. How the judiciary and the press construed history is discussed. Religion enters into the picture in that religion and same-sex marriage were often discussed in light of history. Li was a law student at the time she wrote this book. Smith is an assistant professor of communications at High Point University.

**Miller, Debra A. (2012).** *Gay Marriage.* **Opposing Viewpoints in Context. Farmington Hills, MI: Greenhaven Press.**

This is a good general and fairly widely available book on same-sex marriage. It is a bit dated (published three years before *Obergefell*), but many of the same issues still exist today. One issue highlighted in the book is whether same-sex marriage infringes on religious liberty, and that continues to be a hot button issue today. Miller is the author of a wide variety of books on opposing viewpoints.

**Petro, Anthony Michael. (2015).** *After the Wrath of God: AIDS, Sexuality, and American Religion.* **New York: Oxford University Press.**
This book examines how the AIDS crisis of the 1980s reshaped the debates over sexuality. Petro notes how those on the cultural right have had much staying power in the debate, with great success promoting an abstinence-only education policy, and how many mainstream religions were reshaped by the AIDS crisis. This is important to the issue of same-sex marriage, as many of the same forces in the debate over AIDS were active in the debate over gay marriage nearly 30 years later. Petro is an associate professor of religion and women's, gender, and sexuality studies at Boston University.

**Pierceson, Jason. (2014).** *Same-Sex Marriage in the United States: The Road to the Supreme Court.* **New York: Rowman & Littlefield.**
This work examines the different parts of the country that have registered their opinion on same-sex marriage. It also looks at the political and religious backgrounds. Pierceson goes all the way back to 1950 to set the stage for how the debate started in the early 1990s. A repeated focus is how the issue of federalism shapes the picture. Pierceson is a professor of political science at the University of Illinois, Springfield.

**Rogers, Baker A. (2019).** *Conditionally Accepted: Christians' Perspectives on Sexuality and Gay and Lesbian Civil Rights.* **New Brunswick, NJ: Rutgers University Press.**
This book examines the attitudes of Christians toward gay people, including in the area of same-sex marriage. It also looks at whether having a gay or lesbian friend or relative shapes opinion. It argues that one's place on the religious spectrum is more important than knowing a gay or lesbian. If one is evangelical, one is much more likely to view a gay or lesbian as being in sin, while mainline Protestants are more likely to be supportive, especially to gay or lesbian friends and relatives. Catholics are divided on the issue by how conservative they are, with conservative Catholics viewing the behavior as sin. Rogers is an associate professor of sociology at Georgia Southern University.

**Seymour, Mark, and Sean Brady, eds. (2019).** *From Sodomy Laws to Same-Sex Marriage: International Perspectives since 1789.* **London: Bloomsbury Academic.**

Seymour and Brady have collected a series of essays dealing with same-sex relations since the French Revolution. These essays generally look at the 20th and 21st centuries, although about five of them go back to before 1900. This is truly an international volume, as the topics go from France to Peru to Australia. The authors of the articles are equally international, being from the United Kingdom, New Zealand, and the United States, among other places. Seymour is a professor at the University of Otago in New Zealand, and Brady is a professor at the University of London in the United Kingdom.

**Shilts, Randy. (1994).** *Conduct Unbecoming: Gays and Lesbians in the U.S. Military.* **New York: St. Martins.**

This book looks at the battle over having gay people openly serve in the U.S. military. It covers in-depth the largest civil rights battle for the LGBTQ community before the struggle over same-sex marriage. Many of the same tactics and issues, including religious ones, that are eventually used to win the same-sex marriage battle (and many of the same opponents and tactics) occur here as well. Shilts was one of the leading journalists of the 1970s and 1980s. He wrote for *The Advocate* and many other publications and also authored one of the best treatments on the AIDS epidemic of the early 1980s.

**Taylor, Verta A., and Mary Bernstein, eds. (2013).** *The Marrying Kind?: Debating Same-Sex Marriage within the Lesbian and Gay Movement.* **Minneapolis: University of Minnesota Press.**

Bernstein and Taylor collected a series of essays looking at how the lesbian and gay movement views marriage. Questions within the movement include how desirable is marriage and what effect will broadscale marriage have on the community? Throughout the book is the question of how religion affects all this. Taylor is a professor of sociology at the University of California, Santa Barbara, and Bernstein is a professor of sociology at the University of Connecticut.

**Thompson, Tamara. (2015).** *Same-Sex Marriage.* **Opposing Viewpoints in Context. Greenhaven Press, a part of Gale, Cengage Learning.**

This book provides a snapshot of views on same-sex marriage in 2015, right after the *Obergefell* decision. It gives a history of the road to the decision and then looks at related issues. Some of the topics covered include how society is impacted by same-sex marriage. Families are also considered in terms of how they are affected. Finally, religion is also discussed. This book is part of Greenhaven Press's Opposing Viewpoints in Context series. Thompson is an author and editor of a wide variety of books on current controversies.

**Viefhues-Bailey, Ludger H. (2010).** *Between a Man and a Woman? Why Conservatives Oppose Same-Sex Marriage.* **New York: Columbia University Press.**
Viefhues-Bailey examines why conservatives oppose same-sex marriage. While nostalgia and biblical references are a part, the author holds that there is more to it than that. It looks at documents produced by a variety of conservative groups, including Focus on the Family. Viefhues-Bailey suggests that gender roles play a large part in the opposition of conservative groups to same-sex marriage, as it disrupts those roles nearly as much as it disrupts anything else. Viefhues-Bailey is a distinguished professor of philosophy, gender, and culture at Le Moyne College in Syracuse, New York.

**Whitlow, Julie, and Patricia Ould. (2015).** *Same-Sex Marriage, Context, and Lesbian Identity: Wedded but Not Always a Wife.* **Lanham, MD: Lexington Books.**
This book looks at an interesting effect of same-sex marriage—the terms used for one's spouse. For most opposite-sex couples, the terms are fairly straightforward—the man is the husband, and the woman is the wife—but for opposite-sex couples, it is not as simple. Whitlow and Ould examine lesbian couples to see how and when they choose to use or avoid the term *wife* and how religion plays a role. This book combines interview and survey data to take a linguistic look at the issue. Whitlow is a professor of English, and Ould is a professor of sociology. Both teach at Salem State University in Massachusetts.

**Yarbrough, Michael W., Angela Jones, and Joseph Nicholas DeFilippis, eds. (2019).** *Queer Families and Relationships after Marriage Equality.* **New York: Routledge, Taylor and Francis.**
Yarbrough, Jones, and DeFilippis have collected about a dozen essays that examine how marriage equality has shaped LGBTQ families. They include

stories from all over the world, from South Africa to China, as well as interviews. Yarbrough is an assistant professor of criminal justice at John Jay College in New York City. Angela Jones is an associate professor of sociology at Farmingdale State College. Joseph Nicholas DeFilippis is a professor of social work at Seattle University.

# Index

Page numbers in **bold** indicate main entries.

# About the Author

SCOTT A. MERRIMAN is a lecturer in history at Troy University. He has authored or edited over a dozen books, including *Religion and the Law in America: An Encyclopedia of Personal Belief and Public Policy* (ABC-CLIO) and *When Religious and Secular Interests Collide: Faith, Law, and the Religious Exemption Debate* (Praeger). His first book, *The History Highway*, was a History Book of the Month Club selection. He has been named the Gamma Beta Phi Teacher of the Year at Troy. His research interests include the First Amendment, the Espionage and Sedition Acts, and the intersection of religion and the civil rights movement.